# Family Circle® ABZ's of Cooking

### Edited by Lucy Wing with
### The Family Circle Food Department

# Volume 3

# Introduction

Prepare low-cost chicken, Chinese-style, as pictured on the cover of this volume and you have a real winner! So quick and delicious—just add rice and a dessert for a complete meal. In this volume, we illustrate how to cut up and bone a chicken at home to save you money. Canning fresh fruits and vegetables when they are plentiful and least expensive is another money-saving idea. With this volume, canning is simple to learn.

For those with a sweet tooth, sample the cake, candy, cheesecake and chocolate recipes. Some of the cake recipes are simple to prepare using only one bowl. We include tips on decorating with chocolate as well as a glossary of chocolate products.

Cheese and casserole dishes will add variety to your family meals. Also included is a table of the most popular cheeses. And for children who love to cook, there is an illustrated step-by-step section just for kids. The junior chefs in the family can prepare a full meal all by themselves.

Look under Christmas Food Gifts for make-ahead recipes; many foods can make lovely hostess gifts.

A creative collection of recipes awaits you in this volume.

# Contents

Cover photo: Walnut Chicken, page 182

ISBN 0-8249-9003-X b

Published by Ideals Publishing Corporation
11315 Watertown Plank Road
Milwaukee, WI 53226

**Family Circle Staff**

| | |
|---|---|
| **Project Editor** | Lucy Wing |
| **Food Editor** | Jean Hewitt |
| **Senior Associate Food Editor** | Jane O'Keefe |
| **Art Director** | Joseph Taveroni |
| **Copy Editors** | Karen Saks |
| | Susan Tierney |
| **Project Management** | Annabelle Arenz |
| | John Jaxheimer |

**Ideals Publishing Staff**

| | |
|---|---|
| **Project Editor** | Julie Hogan |
| **Food Stylist** | Susan Noland |
| **Photographer** | Gerald Koser |
| **Project Management** | James Kuse |
| | Marybeth Owens |

**Photographs by:** Avedis, Paul Christensen, Richard Jeffery, Allen Lieberman, Bill McGinn, Rudy Muller, George Nordhausen, Gordon E. Smith, Bob Stoller, Rene Velez

**C**ABBAGE A versatile and inexpensive vegetable that is available year-round. It is a cousin of broccoli, cauliflower, Brussels sprouts and collards. Cabbage is an excellent source of vitamin C and has only 20 calories per 3½-ounce cooked serving.

A variety of cabbage was eaten by the ancient Romans and Greeks, and the Chinese and Koreans have cultivated the vegetable for centuries. Its origin is traced to a wild species that grows in the eastern Mediterranean and western Asian areas.

Cabbage can be eaten fresh or cooked. It can also be preserved by pickling or salting. Sauerkraut is the most popular form of preserved cabbage. For more recipes, see **COLE-SLAW.**

**Buying and Storing**: There are numerous varieties of cabbage available on the market. We can divide the cabbage family into the following types: green, Chinese, red and savoy.

*Green cabbage* is the most common type. Although markets do not identify the different names of green cabbage, you can familiarize yourself with the characteristics of the three most prevalent varieties: *Pointed* is a variety marketed in early spring; it has a conical or pointed head. *Danish,* also called *Hollander,* is a late-maturing, good-storage variety.

*Domestic* has a solid, but not-too-compact, round head.

All types are equally versatile. Depending on variety and season, heads of green cabbage weigh from 1 to 5 pounds. The outer leaves may be pale, bright or silvery green; some heads may be almost white.

The availability of *Chinese cabbage* is increasing in our markets. There are two different varieties: *Bok choy,* also called *Chinese chard,* resembles Swiss chard—it has white stalks with dark green leaves. When buying this type of cabbage, select crisp, firm heads; avoid greenish-white stalks and yellow leaves. You can keep it refrigerated in a plastic bag for up to one week. Use bok choy in stir-fried dishes or add it to soups. The stalks should be cooked longer than the leaves, so cut them into pieces and stir-fry them first. The hearts of bok choy, prized in Chinese cuisine, are usually blanched and served with soy sauce and sesame oil.

Another variety of Chinese cabbage, called *Napa cabbage, celery cabbage* or *pe-tsai,* looks like an elongated head of savoy cabbage. It has pale green to white crinkled leaves, with wide, flat stalks. Select firm, compact heads of Napa cabbage. Refrigerate in a plastic bag and use within one week. Napa cabbage can be stir-fried or added to soups, or shred-

ded for salads. When stir-fried, it should be served immediately; it gets watery if you let it stand.

*Red cabbage* differs from green cabbage only in color. Its rich, purpled-red color makes it a popular addition to salads. To preserve this cabbage's bright red color during cooking, add 1 to 2 tablespoons of lemon juice or cider vinegar, or add a few slices of fresh apple.

*Savoy* is an unusually mild and delicate cabbage, good cooked or raw. The heads are large, with crinkly green leaves. You should look for unblemished heads. Store them refrigerated in a plastic bag. Use within one week.

| Cabbage Math |
|---|
| 1 small head (2 pounds) = 8 cups shredded raw |
| 1 small head (2 pounds) = 4 servings of cooked wedges |

**To Prepare**: Wash cabbage and trim off any wilted leaves. Cut in half through the core or center; cut into wedges or shred finely.

**To Cook**: Cook green cabbage wedges in about 1 inch of boiling water over high heat for 2 minutes; lower heat; cover and cook about 15 minutes or until crisp-tender. Drain and season with salt, pepper, herbs or butter. To sauté or stir-fry shredded cabbage, heat 2 tablespoons butter or

oil in a large skillet. Add about 8 cups shredded cabbage; cook just until wilted. Cover and cook over low heat 2 more minutes or until tender.

**To Microwave:** Use a 10-inch baking dish; arrange cabbage wedges like spokes of a wheel. Add ¼ cup water. Cover with vented plastic wrap. Microwave on high power 7 minutes. Rotate dish; microwave 6 to 8 more minutes. Let stand, covered, 2 minutes. Drain, season and serve.

## CABBAGE BUNDLES IN PAPRIKA CREAM SAUCE

*Delicious little packages filled with inexpensive ground beef plus rice, other ingredients, and bathed in a tasty sour cream sauce.*

Makes 6 to 8 servings.

- 1 head green cabbage (3 to 3½ pounds)
- 2 cups fresh bread crumbs (4 slices)
- 1 teaspoon seasoned salt
- ½ cup cold water
- 1 pound ground chuck
- 2 eggs
- 1 cup cooked rice
- ¼ cup (½ stick) butter or margarine
- 1 medium-size onion, chopped (½ cup)
- 2 carrots, sliced (1 cup)
- 1 tablespoon paprika
- 1 teaspoon salt
- 1 can condensed beef broth
- 1 can (8 ounces) tomato sauce
- 1 tablespoon all-purpose flour
- 1 container (8 ounces) dairy sour cream, at room temperature
  Fresh dill or parsley

1. In a large kettle heat to boiling enough water to cover cabbage. Trim damaged outer leaves from cabbage. Stick a large fork deep into core. Lower the cabbage into boiling water, holding on to fork. With a small sharp knife, loosen and remove 12 to 16 outer leaves as they become soft and pliable; drain. Chop remaining cabbage coarsely (to make 6 cups).
2. Combine crumbs, salt and water in a large bowl; add beef, eggs and rice; mix well. Place about ¼ cup meat

mixture on each leaf; fold sides of leaf over stuffing; roll up from thick end of leaf.
3. Heat butter in large Dutch oven. Add onion; sauté a few minutes; stir in carrots and chopped cabbage; sauté, stirring often, until soft, about 10 minutes. Stir in paprika, salt, broth and tomato sauce. Arrange stuffed cabbage bundles, seam-side down and close together, over cabbage mixture in Dutch oven; cover. Cook over low heat, basting, 50 minutes to 1 hour.
4. Carefully remove cabbage bundles and keep warm. Stir flour into sour cream; add to Dutch oven. Bring slowly to boiling, stirring constantly; boil 1 minute. Layer cabbage mixture and cabbage bundles in heated serving dish. Garnish with fresh dill or parsley.

## STUFFED CABBAGE WITH AVGOLEMONO SAUCE

Bake at 375° for 1 hour, 20 minutes. Makes 8 servings.

- 1 head (3¼ pounds) savoy or green cabbage
- 2 teaspoons salt
- 1 package (7 ounces) beef-flavored rice mix with vermicelli
- 1 pound ground round
- 5 eggs
- 3 tablespoons lemon juice
- ½ cup dry white wine
- ½ cup water
- 1 bay leaf
- 3 sprigs parsley
- 2 teaspoons cornstarch
  Salt
  White pepper

1. Rinse cabbage under cold water; remove and discard damaged leaves. Put cabbage in a large saucepan; add 2 teaspoons salt and water to cover; simmer 15 minutes or until tender. Drain cabbage, reserving 1 cup broth; let stand until cool enough to handle, about 20 minutes. Prepare rice mix, following label directions. Let cool slightly; stir in ground beef, 2 of the eggs and 1 tablespoon of the lemon juice, mixing thoroughly.

2. Preheat oven to 350°. Place cabbage, stem-end down, on a flat surface and gently pull 12 to 14 leaves away from center, one at a time, being careful not to tear them. Using a small, sharp knife, cut out firm heart of inner leaves from the stem. (Inner leaves may be sliced, tossed with a sweet-sour dressing, refrigerated and used as a salad.) Mound 2½ cups of the meat mixture in center of cabbage leaves, shaping into a round ball. Fold 3 or 4 of the leaves up and over meat to enclose, pressing firmly together. Spoon remaining meat mixture around and on top of center leaves, pressing firmly. Gently fold all the remaining leaves back into place, overlapping them to give the cabbage its original rounded shape. (Meat stuffing may show through at top.) Place cabbage, stem-end down, in the center of a large square of cheesecloth; bring edges of cloth together above cabbage and tie tightly. Place in a large deep baking dish that will just fit cabbage. Add white wine, ½ cup water, bay leaf and parsley. Cover baking dish with aluminum foil.
3. Bake in a preheated moderate oven (375°) for 1 hour, 20 minutes, basting after 30 minutes. Remove cabbage from baking dish. Pour juices into a 2-cup measure. (Discard bay leaf and parsley.) Add enough of reserved cabbage broth to measure 1½ cups; pour into a small saucepan; bring to boiling.
4. Beat the remaining 3 eggs, the remaining 2 tablespoons lemon juice and cornstarch in a medium-size bowl. Pour in boiling hot liquid, beating constantly, until thoroughly combined. Return to saucepan and cook over low heat, 5 minutes, stirring constantly, until thickened. (Be careful not to overcook or eggs will curdle.) Remove from heat; taste and add salt and white pepper, if needed.
5. To serve: Unwrap cabbage, cut into wedges; pour some of the sauce over cabbage wedges and pass the rest in a heated gravy boat. Garnish serving platter with cooked carrot sticks, if you wish.

## RED CABBAGE

Makes 6 to 8 servings.

    1  medium-size head red cabbage
       (about 3 pounds)
    1  medium-size onion, sliced
    2  large apples, pared and
       chopped
    1  tablespoon bacon drippings
    1  teaspoon salt
    6  tablespoons sugar
    1  cup cider vinegar
 1½  cups water
   ¼  teaspoon ground allspice
    1  bay leaf
    2  cloves
    6  peppercorns

1. Remove any bruised and discolored outer leaves from cabbage. Quarter and core cabbage. Slice thinly to make about 12 cups. Combine with onion and apples in a large kettle.

2. Add bacon drippings, salt, sugar, vinegar, water and allspice. Tie bay leaf, cloves and peppercorns in a small piece of cheesecloth. Add to cabbage.

3. Cover and simmer 30 minutes; uncover; simmer 1 hour longer. Remove spice bag. Serve hot. This reheats well.

• • •

**CAESAR SALAD** Just the right combination and quality of ingredients give this simple, yet justly famous salad its distinctive taste. It was created by a restaurateur named Caesar Cardini in Tijuana, Mexico, in the early 1920's.

## CAESAR SALAD

Makes 6 servings.

   ¾  cup olive oil
    1  clove garlic, crushed
    3  slices white bread
    3  tablespoons lemon juice
    6  flat anchovy fillets, finely
       chopped
   ½  teaspoon salt
   ½  teaspoon dry mustard
   ⅛  teaspoon pepper
   ½  teaspoon Worcestershire sauce
    1  egg
    1  large head romaine lettuce
   ½  cup freshly grated Parmesan
       cheese

1. Combine olive oil and garlic in cup; let stand several hours or overnight. Remove and discard garlic.

2. Cut bread into small cubes. Heat ¼ cup of the garlic oil in a large skillet. Add bread cubes; spread in a single layer. Sauté, stirring frequently, until golden brown. Drain on paper toweling.

3. Combine the remaining ½ cup garlic oil, lemon juice, anchovies, salt, mustard, pepper and Worcestershire in a large salad bowl.

4. Place egg in small bowl of hot water; let stand 10 minutes or until just at room temperature.

5. Tear romaine leaves into bowl in bite-size pieces, removing any coarse ribs. (You should have about 12 cups, or 3 quarts, torn leaves.)

6. Top greens with half of the Parmesan cheese. Break egg over salad. Toss salad, spooning from bottom of bowl each time, until greens are evenly coated with dressing. Sprinkle with remaining Parmesan cheese and bread cubes. Toss and serve immediately.

• • •

**CAKE** Cake baking is not only an art, but also a science—the proper ingredients in the proper proportions are needed to chemically transform a wet batter into a light, airy product. There are two types of cakes: butter and foam.

*Butter cakes,* such as pound cakes, fruitcakes, chocolate or spice cakes, are made of butter or vegetable shortening, sugar, flour and a leavening agent and can be shaped into round layers, loaves or cupcakes. Some tortes, usually made of many layers and a rich filling or frosting, are also considered butter cakes. For more recipes, see **CHOCOLATE, CUPCAKE, FRUITCAKE, TORTE.**

*Foam cakes* rely on air beaten into egg whites as the leavening agent, although some baking powder may also be added. Angel food cakes, for example, are made only with egg

## HIGH ALTITUDE TIPS FOR CAKES

Most cake recipes are developed for altitudes from sea level up to 3,000 feet. Above that, it is often necessary to adjust the proportions of certain ingredients, usually a decrease in leavening or sugar or both and an increase in the amount of liquid. Make the following adjustments for high altitudes:

| Altitude | 3,000-4,000' | 4,000-6,000' | 6,000-7,500' |
|---|---|---|---|
| *Reduce Baking Powder* For each teaspoon, decrease | ⅛ tsp. | ⅛ to ¼ tsp. | ¼ tsp. |
| *Reduce Sugar* For each cup, decrease | 1 tbs. | 1-2 tbs. | 3-4 tbs. |
| *Increase Liquid* For each cup, add | 1-2 tbs. | 2-4 tbs. | 3-4 tbs. |
| *Increase Baking Temperature* | 25° | 25° | 25° |

● For particularly rich butter or shortening cakes, try reducing the shortening by 1 or 2 tablespoons.

● If you live at an extremely high altitude, you may wish to increase the amount of egg in angel food, chiffon or sponge cakes.

● Only by experimenting will you find the right modifications for your needs. Try the smaller adjustments on any recipe the first time you make it; then, next time, if necessary, make larger adjustment.

Pictured opposite: Coconut Marmalade Cake, page 136

# Cake

whites, sugar, cake flour and a flavoring. No butter or oil or additional leavening agent is used. Chiffon cakes on the other hand, are made with egg yolks and oil mixed into the batter; then the batter is folded into beaten egg whites. Sponge cakes, which include jelly-roll cakes, are made by beating the whole eggs with sugar until thick, then gradually folding in a mixture of cake flour, baking powder and salt. For more recipes, see **SPONGE CAKE.**

### How to Frost a Cake

1. Place the cake plate on something you can turn—a lazy Susan, if you have one. Or, set plate on a large, inverted bowl or a sugar canister. Then rotate the plate as you frost the cake.
2. Before frosting the cake, brush off all loose crumbs.
3. When frosting layer cakes, put flat bottoms of cake together, facing one another. This way the cake will be steady and level.
4. Frost the entire outside of the assembled cake with a *very thin layer of frosting;* let it set about 20 minutes. The thin coating holds the crumbs in place and keeps them from mixing with the final coat of frosting.
5. Frost the sides of the cake first from bottom up, then top, swirling frosting into soft peaks.

## COCONUT MARMALADE CAKE

Bake at 375° for 25 minutes.
Makes one three-layer 8-inch cake.

- 1½ cups *sifted* cake flour
- 1 teaspoon baking powder
- ½ teaspoon salt
- 6 eggs, separated
- ½ teaspoon cream of tartar
- 1½ cups sugar
- ⅓ cup water
- 1 teaspoon vanilla
  10X (confectioners') sugar
- 1 jar (18 ounces) orange marmalade or peach jam
  White Mountain Frosting *(recipe follows)*
- 1 can (3½ or 4 ounces) coconut

1. Grease bottoms of a 15½ × 10½ × 1-inch jelly-roll pan and two 8 × 1½-inch layer pans; line with wax paper; grease again. Flour all pans lightly, tapping out excess. Preheat oven to 375°.
2. Sift the flour, baking powder and salt onto wax paper.
3. Beat egg whites and cream of tartar in large bowl with electric mixer at high speed until foamy white and doubled in volume. Beat in ½ cup of the sugar, slowly, until meringue stands in soft peaks.
4. Beat egg yolks in small bowl with mixer at high speed until thick and lemon-colored. Beat in the remaining 1 cup sugar, gradually, until mixture is very thick and fluffy. Beat in the water and vanilla at low speed.
5. Fold flour mixture into egg yolk mixture until completely blended.
6. Fold yolk mixture into meringue until no white streaks remain.
7. Measure 4 cups batter into prepared jelly-roll pan, spreading evenly into corners; divide remaining batter evenly into layer-cake pans. Place jelly-roll pan on lower shelf in oven, cake layers on middle shelf.
8. Bake in a preheated moderate oven (375°) for 15 minutes. Reverse pans in oven and continue baking for 10 minutes or until tops spring back when lightly pressed with fingertip.
9. As soon as cakes are done, loosen around sides of pans with knife; invert oblong cake onto a clean towel dusted with 10X (confectioners') sugar; peel off wax paper. Roll up with towel; let cool 10 minutes. Invert cake layers onto racks. Peel off wax paper; cool layers.
10. Unroll oblong cake; spread with 1 cup of the jam. Divide remaining jam between the tops of the round cake layers.
11. Place one cake layer, jam-side up, on serving plate. Cut oblong cake lengthwise into 8 strips, each 1¼-inches wide. (Measure with ruler so strips will be even.) Roll up one strip, jelly-roll fashion; lay flat on center of cake layer on serving plate. Matching ends, wind remaining strips, one at a time, around roll to make a big pinwheel. Place second cake layer, jam-side down, on the pinwheel to make three layers.

12. Prepare frosting. Frost sides, then top of cake. Press coconut onto sides and top of cake while still moist. Chill several hours. Cut with sharp knife dipped in hot water.

## WHITE MOUNTAIN FROSTING

Makes enough to frost two or three 8-inch cake layers.

- ½ cup sugar
- ¼ cup light corn syrup
- 2 tablespoons water
- 2 egg whites
- ⅛ teaspoon cream of tartar
- ½ teaspoon vanilla

1. Combine sugar, corn syrup and water in a small saucepan; cover. Heat to boiling; uncover; boil gently, without stirring, until mixture registers 242° on a candy thermometer or until a small amount of the hot syrup falls, threadlike, from spoon.
2. While syrup cooks, beat egg whites with cream of tartar in a large bowl with electric mixer until stiff peaks form when beaters are removed. Pour hot syrup into egg whites in a very thin stream, beating all the time at high speed, until frosting is stiff and glossy. Beat in the vanilla.

## GREAT-GRANDMA'S SOFT GINGER CAKE

Bake at 350° for 30 minutes.
Makes one 13 × 9-inch cake.

- 2½ cups *sifted* all-purpose flour
- 1¾ teaspoons baking soda
- 1 teaspoon ground ginger
- 1 teaspoon ground cinnamon
- ¼ teaspoon ground cloves
- ¼ teaspoon salt
- 1 cup sugar
- ½ cup vegetable shortening
- 1 cup molasses
- 1 cup boiling water
- 2 eggs, well beaten

1. Sift together flour, soda, ginger, cinnamon, cloves and salt; set aside.
2. Cream sugar with shortening and molasses until well blended. Preheat oven to 350°.
3. Add sifted dry ingredients to creamed mixture alternately with boiling water, beginning and ending

# Cake

with dry ingredients. Stir in eggs.

4. Pour into a well-greased 13 × 9 × 2-inch baking pan.

5. Bake in a preheated moderate oven (350°) for 30 minutes or until center springs back when lightly pressed with fingertip. Cool in pan on wire rack to room temperature. Cut in large squares.

## COLONIAL SEED CAKE

Bake at 350° for 1 hour, 15 minutes.
Makes one loaf cake.

- **1 jar (2 ounces) poppy seeds (½ cup)**
- **¾ cup milk**
- **¾ cup (1½ sticks) soft butter**
- **3 eggs**
- **1¼ cups sugar**
- **1 teaspoon vanilla**
- **2 teaspoons baking powder**
- **2 cups** *sifted* **all-purpose flour**
  **10X (confectioners') sugar**

1. Combine poppy seeds and milk in a large bowl. Let stand at room temperature 3 to 4 hours. Let butter and eggs warm to room temperature for easy mixing. (Butter should be *very* soft.) Grease and flour an 8½ × 4½ × 2½-inch loaf pan. Preheat oven to 350°.

2. Add butter, eggs, sugar, vanilla, baking powder and flour to poppy seeds and milk. Beat at medium speed with electric mixer for 1 minute, scraping side of bowl with plastic spatula. Pour into prepared pan.

3. Bake in a preheated moderate oven (350°) for 1 hour and 15 minutes or until center springs back when lightly pressed with fingertip. Cool in pan on wire rack 5 minutes. Loosen around edges; turn out to cool. Sprinkle with 10X sugar. Serve plain or with whipped cream, if you wish.

## PEANUT BUTTER CAKE

Bake at 350° for 45 minutes, then at 325° for 20 minutes.
Makes one 12-cup Bundt cake.

- **¾ cup (1½ sticks) butter**
- **¼ cup creamy peanut butter**
- **4 eggs**
- **½ cup buttermilk**
- **2 cups sugar**
- **3 teaspoons baking powder**
- **3 cups** *sifted* **all-purpose flour**
- **1 teaspoon vanilla**
- **½ cup water**
  **Peanut Butter Topping** *(recipe follows)*

1. Let butter, peanut butter, eggs and buttermilk warm to room temperature for easy mixing. (Butter should be *very* soft.) Grease and flour a 12-cup Bundt pan or a 10-inch tube pan. Preheat oven to 350°.

2. Combine room temperature ingredients with sugar, baking powder, flour, vanilla and water in a large bowl. Beat at slow speed with electric mixer for 30 seconds, then at medium speed for 2 minutes, scraping side of bowl. Pour into prepared pan.

3. Bake in a preheated moderate oven (350°) for 45 minutes, then lower heat to 325° and bake 20 minutes longer or until top springs back when lightly pressed with fingertip. Cool on wire rack 10 minutes. Turn out; cool completely before frosting.

**Peanut Butter Topping:** Combine ¼ cup creamy peanut butter, 1 cup 10X (confectioners') sugar and 4 to 5 tablespoons buttermilk in small bowl until smooth. Spoon over cake.

## MISSISSIPPI MUD CAKE

*Candy bars frost this easy cake.*
Bake at 350° for 40 minutes.
Makes one 11¾ × 7½-inch cake.

- **¾ cup (1½ sticks) butter**
- **½ cup heavy cream**
- **½ cup brewed coffee**
- **4 eggs**
- **1½ cups sugar**
- **½ cup cocoa**
- **1¾ cups** *sifted* **all-purpose flour**
- **2 teaspoons baking powder**
- **½ teaspoon salt**
- **1 teaspoon vanilla**
- **4 bars (1.2 ounces each) milk chocolate candy**

1. Let butter, cream, coffee and eggs warm to room temperature for easy mixing. (Butter should be *very* soft.) Grease and flour an 11¾ × 7½ × 1¾-inch baking pan. Preheat oven to 350°.

2. Combine room temperature ingredients with remaining ingredients, except candy bars, in a large bowl.

Beat at medium speed with electric mixer for 1 minute, scraping side of bowl with plastic spatula. Pour into prepared pan.

3. Bake in a preheated moderate oven (350°) for 40 minutes or until center springs back when lightly pressed with fingertip. Place on wire rack.

4. Break chocolate bars into pieces; place on hot cake; let stand 1 minute, then spread softened chocolate with spatula to frost cake. Cool before serving.

## BOURBON APPLESAUCE CAKE

*Moist and delicious, this cake keeps very well.*
Bake at 325° for 1 hour, 30 minutes.
Makes one loaf cake.

- **½ cup (1 stick) butter**
- **2 eggs**
- **1 cup firmly packed brown sugar**
- **2½ cups** *sifted* **all-purpose flour**
- **2 teaspoons baking soda**
- **¼ teaspoon salt**
- **¼ cup wheat germ**
- **2 cups sweetened applesauce**
- **¼ cup bourbon or apple cider**
- **¾ cup finely chopped walnuts**
  **10X (confectioners') sugar**

1. Let butter and eggs warm to room temperature for easy mixing. (Butter should be *very* soft.) Grease and flour a 9 × 5 × 3-inch loaf pan. Preheat oven to 325°.

2. Combine room temperature ingredients with brown sugar, flour, baking soda, salt, wheat germ, applesauce and bourbon or cider in a large bowl. Beat at medium speed with electric mixer for 3 minutes, scraping down side of bowl with plastic spatula. Stir in nuts. Pour into prepared pan.

3. Bake in a preheated slow oven (325°) for 1 hour and 30 minutes or until center springs back when lightly pressed with fingertip. Cool in pan on wire rack 10 minutes. Loosen around edges with metal spatula; remove from pan. Cool completely. Sprinkle with 10X sugar.

*Note:* Spoon an additional ¼ cup bourbon or apple cider over cake while it is still warm, if you wish.

# Cake

## ORANGE CHIFFON CAKE

*Truly an all-American variety, the chiffon cake is one of the best of the sponge-type cakes to come along in this century. It was created in the 1930's following the development of the angel food cake.*

Bake at 325° for 1 hour, 10 minutes.
Makes one 10-inch cake.

- 2½ cups *sifted* cake flour
- 1⅓ cups sugar
- 3 teaspoons baking powder
- ¼ teaspoon salt
- ½ cup vegetable oil
- 5 egg yolks
- ½ cup water
- 2 tablespoons grated orange rind
- ¼ cup orange juice
- 7 to 8 egg whites (1 cup)
- ½ teaspoon cream of tartar
  Orange Glaze (recipe follows)

1. Sift flour, 1 cup of the sugar, baking powder and salt into a medium-size bowl. Make a well in center and add *in order:* oil, egg yolks, water, orange rind and orange juice; beat with a spoon until smooth. Preheat oven to 325°.
2. Beat egg whites and cream of tartar in a large bowl with electric mixer on high speed until foamy white and doubled in volume. Gradually beat in remaining sugar until meringue stands in firm peaks.
3. Pour egg yolk mixture over beaten egg white mixture; fold mixture gently until no streaks of white remain. Pour batter into an ungreased 10-inch tube pan.
4. Bake in a preheated slow oven (325°) for 1 hour and 10 minutes or until top springs back when lightly pressed with fingertip.
5. Invert pan on funnel or soda bottle to keep top of cake off countertop; let cake cool completely upside down. When cool, loosen cake around the tube and down the side with spatula. Remove from pan. Drizzle with Orange Glaze or sprinkle with 10X sugar and serve with fresh fruits, if you wish.

**Orange Glaze:** Combine 1 cup 10X (confectioners') sugar with 2 tablespoons orange juice in a small bowl until smooth.

## SOUR CREAM MARBLE POUND CAKE

*Rich chocolate swirls through this sour cream pound cake.*

Bake at 350° for 1 hour, 30 minutes.
Makes one 9-inch tube cake.

- 3 cups *sifted* all-purpose flour
- 1 teaspoon baking soda
- ½ teaspoon salt
- 1 cup (2 sticks) butter
- 3 cups sugar
- ½ teaspoon almond extract
- 6 eggs
- 1 container (8 ounces) dairy sour cream
- 2 squares unsweetened chocolate, melted and cooled

1. Grease and flour a 9-inch tube pan.
2. Sift flour, baking soda and salt onto wax paper. Preheat oven to 350°.
3. Beat butter and sugar in a large bowl with electric mixer until well mixed. Beat in almond extract. Add eggs, one at a time, beating at high speed until mixture is light and fluffy.
4. Stir in ⅓ of the flour mixture, then half the sour cream; repeat, ending with flour. Divide batter in half. Mix one part with the melted chocolate.
5. Spoon half the plain batter into prepared pan. Pour chocolate batter over, then top with remaining plain batter. Pull a spatula in a zigzag motion through batter to marbleize. Do not overmix.
6. Bake in a preheated moderate oven (350°) for 1 hour and 30 minutes or until top springs back when touched lightly with fingertip.
7. Cool in pan on wire rack 10 minutes. Loosen cake around the side with spatula. Remove side of pan by lifting cake out with tube; let cake cool completely on wire rack. Remove cake from tube and bottom; wrap in foil and let stand at room temperature overnight before slicing.

———— ●●● ————

**CAMEMBERT** This small, round, soft cheese is named after a village in Normandy, France. It is made from cow's milk and ripens after its surface has been sprayed with a white mold.

Camembert was supposedly developed in 1790 by a woman named Madame Harel, whose recipe was passed on to her descendants. However, records show that the cheese apparently existed as early as the 12th century.

Cheeses called "Camembert" are made in many countries, including the United States. Camembert is essentially a dessert cheese which should be eaten at room temperature. It should be soft but not runny; if it is shrunken or smells of ammonia, it is past its prime.

**CANAPÉ** A small, decorative, open-face "sandwich" served with cocktails. Canapés may be cut or shaped in a variety of attractive ways. You can use many foods for the base of canapés—as the base of the sandwich—bread, crackers, split tiny cream puffs, even sliced cucumbers. The base is spread with butter or mayonnaise before being topped with different tidbits. Almost any garnish can be used. See **APPETIZERS.**

## PARTY CANAPÉS

*These appetizers can be made ahead and frozen to have on hand.*

Makes 2 dozen.

- ¼ cup (½ stick) butter or margarine, softened
- 1 package (3 ounces) cream cheese, softened
- ½ teaspoon Worcestershire sauce
- 2 hard-cooked eggs
- 3 slices white bread
- 3 slices whole-wheat bread
  Various garnishes

1. Blend butter or margarine, cream cheese and Worcestershire sauce until smooth in a medium-size bowl; spoon half into a second bowl.
2. Halve eggs; remove yolks; press through a sieve and blend into mixture in one bowl. Cover bowl and set aside with whites for decorating canapés.
3. Trim crusts from bread; cut 12 rounds out with 1½-inch cutter from 3 slices; cut 12 diamond shapes from remaining slices. Spread each with plain cheese mixture. Decorate with various garnishes as directed next page.

Pictured opposite: (Clockwise from the top) Peanut Butter Cake, page 137; Mississippi Mud Cake, page 137; Colonial Seed Cake, page 137; Bourbon Applesauce Cake, page 137

# Canapé

## PARTY CANAPÉS

### How to Decorate and Freeze Canapés

- *To Decorate:* Fill a cake-decorating bag with cream-cheese-egg mixture; fit with star tip; pipe an edging around each canapé.
- *To Garnish:* Arrange on each canapé any of the following: small whole shrimp, slivers of rolled smoked salmon, bits of king crab meat or lobster, sliced stuffed green olives or ripe olives, capers, cut-up gherkins, diced pimiento, small pickled onions or diced cooked egg whites.
- *To Freeze:* Place in a single layer in a large, shallow pan; cover tightly with plastic wrap; freeze. Pack in boxes no more than 2 layers deep with plastic wrap between layers. Use canapés within 2 weeks.
- *To Thaw:* Remove canapés from freezer 1 hour before serving; place in a single layer; let stand at room temperature.

——— ●●● ———

**CANDY** The first sweets ever made were probably dried fruits, nuts, seeds and spices mixed with a bit of honey. Egyptians, Arabs and Chinese all made confections with those ingredients. The word candy derives from the Persian word, *qand*. The Persians are also credited with spreading their knowledge of growing, refining and processing sugar cane.

It wasn't until the 14th century that sugar came into wide use in European confections. Only the wealthy could afford candy. Now that sugar is plentiful, you can make and enjoy candy in any of hundreds of variations. Making candy at home is not difficult. Just follow our helpful tips and enjoy the recipes for quick and easy candies. For other recipes, see **BRITTLE** and **FUDGE**.

### Helpful Hints for Making Candy

- Don't attempt to make candies on a hot or humid day. Cool, dry days are best.
- Use a heavy saucepan for more even heat. Remember that the candy might bubble up, so use a pan that's 2 to 3 times larger than the mixture.
- Don't substitute ingredients.
- Don't stir sugar mixture after it comes to a boil, unless it has butter, milk or molasses in it—then stir, or it might burn or boil over.
- To prevent sticky counters, have a bowl of hot water next to the stove to plunge utensils into as they are used.
- To clean saucepan and equipment, boil all together in a larger pot of water—hardened syrup will boil away in a few minutes.
- Sugar cooks in definite stages. It must be watched carefully and removed from heat at the right time. A candy thermometer is a must if you want perfect candy every time, although experienced cooks can tell when candy is done by observing a teaspoon of syrup dropped into cold water.

## JELLY CANDIES

*Pretty, light textured candies with a tart-sweet flavor.*

Makes 40 candies.

- **3 envelopes unflavored gelatin**
- **2 cups sugar**
- **1 cup water**
- **8 drops yellow food coloring**
- **2 tablespoons grated orange rind**

## TEMPERATURES FOR CANDY

| Type of Candy | Temperature on Candy Thermometer (at Sea Level) Degrees F. | Test | Description of Test |
|---|---|---|---|
| Sugar Syrup | 230° to 234° | Thread | Syrup spins a 2-inch thread when dropped from fork or spoon. |
| Fondant, Fudge | 234° to 240° | Soft ball | Syrup, when dropped into very cold water, forms a soft ball that flattens on removal from water. |
| Caramels | 244° to 248° | Firm ball | Syrup, when dropped into very cold water, forms a firm ball that does not flatten on removal from water. |
| Divinity, Marshmallows, some Taffy | 250° to 266° | Hard ball | Syrup, when dropped into very cold water, forms a ball that is hard enough to hold its shape, yet is still plastic. |
| Taffy | 270° to 290° | Soft crack | Syrup, when dropped into very cold water, separates into threads that are hard but not brittle. |
| Brittle, Glacé | 300° to 310° | Hard crack | Syrup, when dropped into very cold water, separates into threads that are hard and brittle. |

1 tablespoon grated lemon rind
¼ cup orange juice
2 tablespoons lemon juice
Sugar for coating

1. Combine gelatin and sugar in a large saucepan; stir in water. Heat to boiling over medium heat, stirring constantly. Lower heat; boil mixture slowly for 20 minutes.

2. Remove pan from heat; add food coloring, orange and lemon rinds and juices. Stir for 2 to 3 minutes, then strain into a well-oiled 9 × 5 × 3-inch pan. Refrigerate until firm, about 4 hours.

3. Loosen around sides with a spatula; turn out onto lightly oiled cookie sheet. Cut into 1-inch cubes by pressing a large sharp knife down through jelly—do not draw through.

4. Toss jelly squares in granulated sugar to coat. Dry overnight on wire racks. Store in tightly covered container. Will stay moist for approximately two weeks at room temperature.

## NEAPOLITAN JELLIES

*Jewel-bright colors in this easy, tender tri-layered confection.*

Makes about 8 dozen.

  6 envelopes unflavored
    gelatin
  4 cups sugar
2⅓ cups water
 ⅓ cup red cinnamon candies
    Marshmallows *(recipe follows)*
 ⅓ cup green crème de menthe
    liqueur
    Granulated sugar

1. Combine 3 envelopes of the gelatin and 2 cups of the sugar in a large saucepan. Stir in 1⅓ cups of the water. Cook mixture over medium heat, stirring constantly, until mixture comes to boiling. Stir in cinnamon candies until they dissolve. Simmer over low heat 20 minutes. Remove from heat.

2. Spoon off foam from surface. Pour jelly into a well-oiled 13 × 9 × 2-inch pan. Chill until firm, about 2 hours.

3. Prepare Marshmallows recipe following *only* steps 2 and 3. Wipe off any excess oil from surface of jelly layer with paper toweling; spread marshmallow evenly over jelly layer. Chill until firm, about 2 hours.

4. Combine the remaining 3 envelopes gelatin and 2 cups sugar in large saucepan. Stir in 1 cup water. Cook mixture over medium heat, stirring constantly, until mixture boils. Stir in crème de menthe. Simmer over low heat 20 minutes. Skim off any foam; cool jelly long enough so that it can be spooned carefully over marshmallow layer without melting it completely. You will get some blending in of the layers. Chill until firm.

5. Run spatula around sides of candy to loosen. Sprinkle top with sugar to coat evenly. Place inverted cookie sheet over pan; holding pan and sheet, turn to unmold candy. Cut into 4 strips lengthwise by pressing knife down through candy but do not pull or draw knife. Cut strips crosswise into ½-inch pieces, wiping knife clean occasionally. Roll candies in sugar. Place on wire rack over wax paper to dry overnight. When dry, store in tightly covered container.

## MARSHMALLOWS

*Candy-pan magic! Simple ingredients unfold before your eyes into fluffy white confections.*

Makes about 4 dozen.

 ½ cup cornstarch
 ½ cup *sifted* 10X (confectioners')
    sugar
  2 envelopes unflavored gelatin
 ½ cup granulated sugar
 ⅓ cup water
 ⅔ cup light corn syrup
 ½ teaspoon vanilla

1. Combine cornstarch and 10X sugar in a small bowl. Butter an 8 × 8 × 2-inch baking pan; sprinkle with some of the cornstarch mixture. (You will be using all the mixture eventually.)

2. Combine gelatin and granulated sugar in a small saucepan; stir in the water. Heat mixture over low heat, stirring constantly, until sugar and gelatin are dissolved.

3. Pour gelatin mixture into a large bowl; add corn syrup and vanilla. Beat with electric mixer on high speed for 15 minutes or until mixture is thick and fluffy. (A stand-up mixer, if you have one, makes the job easier.)

4. Pour marshmallow mixture into prepared pan; smooth top surface with a spatula. Refrigerate overnight to firm.

5. Sieve some cornstarch mixture over the chilled marshmallow mixture. Loosen mixture from sides of pan and turn out onto a cookie sheet sprinkled with cornstarch mixture. Marshmallows will be sticky until thoroughly coated.

6. Cut marshmallow mixture into 1-inch squares with a large sharp knife. Cut straight down in one motion rather than pulling the knife through. Roll each marshmallow in remaining cornstarch mix; dry on wire racks. Will stay moist in a tightly covered container about 3 weeks.

## QUICK AND EASY FUDGE

*A foolproof fudge that turns out right in any kind of weather.*

Makes about 2½ pounds.

3⅓ cups sugar
1⅓ cups evaporated milk
  1 package (12 ounces) semisweet
    chocolate pieces
  3 cups miniature marshmallows
  1 cup chopped walnuts
  1 cup candied red cherries,
    quartered

1. Line an 8 × 8 × 2-inch pan with foil; butter foil.

2. Combine sugar and milk in a medium-size saucepan. Cook over medium heat, stirring constantly, until sugar is dissolved and mixture comes to boiling. Boil, stirring constantly, 5 minutes.

3. Remove from heat; beat in chocolate and marshmallows with wooden spoon. Stir until mixture thickens; stir in nuts and cherries. Pour into prepared pan; let stand until cool and firm.

4. Turn out onto cutting board; remove foil; cut fudge into 1-inch squares. Store in tightly covered container.

## ORANGE CANDIED NUTS

Bake at 250° for 5 minutes, then for 1 hour.
Makes 3 cups.

- **3 cups walnut or pecan halves**
- **2 tablespoons butter or margarine**
- **3 tablespoons orange juice**
- **½ cup sugar**
- **¼ cup grated orange rind**
- **1 teaspoon grated lemon rind**
- **½ cup light corn syrup**

1. Place nuts in a 13 × 9 × 2-inch baking pan. Heat in a slow oven (250°) for 5 minutes.
2. Melt butter in a medium-size saucepan. Stir in orange juice, ¼ cup of the sugar, orange and lemon rinds and corn syrup, stirring constantly. Bring to boiling over medium heat. Boil, without stirring, for 5 minutes. Pour syrup over nuts, stirring constantly, to coat evenly.
3. Bake in a slow oven (250°) for 1 hour, stirring several times. Sprinkle with the remaining ¼ cup sugar; do not stir. Immediately spread out onto greased cookie sheets and separate into individual nuts with two forks; cool. Store in a tightly covered container for up to 3 weeks.

## OLD-FASHIONED CHOCOLATE FUDGE

*A marvelous, melt-in-your-mouth chocolate fudge recipe.*
Makes about 2 pounds.

- **1½ cups milk**
- **4 squares unsweetened chocolate (4 ounces)**
- **4 cups sugar**
- **3 tablespoons light corn syrup**
- **¼ teaspoon salt**
- **1½ teaspoons vanilla**
- **3 tablespoons butter or margarine**

1. Combine milk and chocolate in medium-size heavy saucepan; cook over low heat until chocolate is melted. Add sugar, corn syrup and salt and cook, stirring constantly, to boiling.
2. Cook without stirring to 234° on a candy thermometer. (A teaspoonful of syrup will form a soft ball when dropped in cold water.) Remove from heat at once. Add vanilla and butter, but do not stir in.
3. Leave thermometer in pan while fudge is cooling. Let mixture cool to 110°. When cool enough, you can rest bottom of pan comfortably on hand. Beat with wooden spoon until mixture thickens and just begins to lose its gloss. Mixture will lighten in color as you beat. Beating will take about 15 minutes.
4. Spread in a buttered 8 × 8 × 2-inch pan. Let stand until set and cool; cut into squares.

## FRENCH CHOCOLATE TRUFFLES

*A classic French sweet, and a specialty in northern Italy, where they are served in little fluted cups with pungent espresso.*

Makes about 2 dozen.

- **3 squares unsweetened chocolate**
- **⅓ cup butter or margarine, softened**
- **1¼ cups *sifted* 10X (confectioners') sugar**
- **4 egg yolks**
- **1 teaspoon vanilla**
  **Cocoa, coconut or ground nuts**

1. Melt chocolate in top of double boiler over hot, not boiling, water; cool slightly.
2. Combine butter and 10X sugar in medium-size bowl; beat until smooth. Beat in egg yolks, one at a time. Stir in the cooled chocolate and the vanilla. Chill until mixture is firm enough to handle.
3. Shape into 1-inch balls. Roll in cocoa, coconut or nuts. Place on cookie sheet to set. Store in tightly covered container in refrigerator for not more than 1 week.

## ROCKY ROADS

*Simple and delicious.*
Makes about 1½ pounds.

- **1 pound rich milk chocolate, coarsely chopped**
- **1 cup broken pecans or walnuts**
- **1 cup miniature marshmallows**

1. Melt chocolate in top of double boiler over hot, not boiling, water.

Stir mixture until smooth. Remove from heat; spoon half the mixture into an 8 × 8 × 2-inch foil-lined pan; spread to edges. Return remaining chocolate to the heat.
2. Sprinkle nuts and marshmallows over chocolate in pan. Spoon the remaining chocolate over top. Let stand at room temperature until firm.
3. Turn out onto cutting board; remove foil. Cut candy into pieces. Candy will stay fresh several weeks if left in one piece and wrapped in foil.

## EASY CHOCOLATE PEANUT CLUSTERS

Makes about 2 dozen.

- **2 packages (4 ounces each) sweet cooking chocolate**
- **⅔ cup sweetened condensed milk**
- **1 cup unsalted peanuts, lightly toasted**

1. Melt chocolate in top of double boiler over hot, not boiling water; stir until smooth. Remove from heat; blend in condensed milk and peanuts.
2. Drop by teaspoonfuls onto cookie sheet. Let stand at room temperature until firm, about 2 hours. Store in tightly covered container.

## BASKET OF "FRUIT" CANDIES

Makes 1 pound.

- **1 package (3 ounces) cream cheese, softened**
- **3 to 3½ cups *sifted* 10X (confectioners') sugar**
- **3 drops almond extract**
  **Red and yellow food coloring**
  **Whole cloves and green gumdrops**

Mix cream cheese and sugar in medium-size bowl with wooden spoon until well blended. Stir in almond extract. Divide in thirds. Color one part pink, one part yellow. Mix yellow and red coloring to make the third part orange. Shape into strawberries, bananas and oranges. Roll oranges and strawberries on smallest holes of a grater for texture. Insert a clove into each orange; slice gum drops and use as tops for strawberries. Refrigerate.

● ● ●

*Pictured opposite: Jelly Candies (in lower section of glass), page 140; Neapolitan Jellies, page 141; Quick and Easy Fudge, page 141*

**ABZ's of Cooking** 143

# Canning

**CANNING** Why spend a big chunk of your winter's food budget on fresh fruits or vegetables? Instead, take advantage of summer's bounty all year long by canning the fruits of the harvest.

Canning as a method of preserving food was developed in the mid-19th century. The first food to be canned was milk. It was condensed and sweetened, then placed in a can which was sealed and heated to kill any organisms that might cause spoilage. Since canned foods had an indefinite shelf life and could be transported easily—the process was viewed as a major breakthrough for the food industry.

Home-canning is based on the same principles that the original canning methods were based on, with glass jars replacing cans. The food you are preserving determines the canning and/or processing method. Most filled jars of food are "processed," or heated to the specific temperature necessary to destroy all the bacteria in the food. Some pickles, relishes, jams and jellies do not need to be processed.

Acid foods—tomatoes, vegetables in vinegary liquids, and most fruits—are processed in a water-bath canner. These foods are sterilized at 212°F., which is the boiling point of water at sea level. Non-acid vegetables, meats, fish and poultry all require pressure canning. Only a pressure canner can reach the temperature of 240° F.—which is necessary to destroy the harmful organisms in these foods.

## Equipment Needed For Canning

**Jars**: Standard glass home-canning jars, also called Mason jars. Available in sizes from ½ pint to ½ gallon. These are specially manufactured to withstand extreme heat and cold and have closures that seal tightly. *WARNING: Do not use empty commercial food jars or their lids.*

**Closures**: *Two-piece vacuum cap and lid*—most commonly used type. Consists of flat metal lid with flanged edge, with rubber-like sealing compound on underside. Threaded metal screw band fits over rim of jar to hold lid in place.

*Zinc cap with porcelain liner*—older style closure for jars with threads. Porcelain on inside of cap prevents food from coming into contact with zinc. Damaged liners must be discarded.

*Wire bail with glass lid*—old-fashioned closure. Fits on old jars (or reproductions of them) with glass ledge on which a rubber ring rests. Domed glass lid sets over rim of jar and one rubber ring. Lid is held in place by wire clamp with two loops.

**Steam-pressure canner**: Heavy kettle with lid which is clamped or locked to create a steam-tight seal. It comes with either a dial or a weighted gauge.

**Hot water-bath canner**: Large kettle with tight-fitting cover and metal basket to prevent jars from touching bottom and from bumping each other. (Or, you can use any kettle you have that's large enough for this purpose, plus basket and cover.)

**Jar funnel**: Specially designed for canning, this wide-mouth funnel prevents spillage onto sealing surfaces.

**Jar lifter**: For lifting jars out of canner; has non-slip surface for sure grip.

**Miscellaneous equipment**: Slotted and wooden spoons; chopping, paring knives; vegetable parer; food brushes; colander or strainer; timer.

## Methods of Canning

*Water-Bath Method:* Suitable for high acid foods such as fruits, tomatoes, relishes, pickles. This method processes foods in boiling water (212°). This temperature, over a time period specified in the recipe, is sufficient to destroy the spoilage-causing micro-organisms in acidic foods. The canner must be deep enough for water to cover tops of jars 2 to 4 inches without boiling over.

*Steam-Pressure Method:* Used for low-acid foods such as beets, corn, beans and cabbage, which need a much higher water temperature (240°) to destroy bacteria spores that cause botulism. Use a steam-pressure canner especially designed for higher temperatures. It is essential to follow manufacturer's directions carefully.

## General Directions for Canning with Hot Water-Bath Canner

1. Place hot water-bath canner on surface burner; add water to half fill canner; cover; bring water to boiling while preparing food and jars.
2. Wash jars in hot sudsy water; rinse well, leave in hot water until ready to use.
3. Place lids and screw metal rings in hot sudsy water; rinse well; leave in hot water until ready to use.
4. Follow individual recipe directions carefully. Do not take any shortcuts.
5. Remove jars from water one at a time; drain on paper toweling or clean cloth.
6. Pack and/or ladle food into jars, using a wide-mouth funnel, leaving the required head space, ¼ to ½ inch.
7. Remove any air bubbles by running a thin wooden or plastic spoon handle or other thin non-metallic utensil around between the food and jar. A metal utensil might nick the jar.
8. Wipe top and threads of each jar with a clean cloth; place lid on top; screw metal rings on tightly, but do not use force.
9. Place jars in canner rack and lower into rapidly boiling water. Add additional boiling water to kettle if level of water is not 2 inches above jars; cover kettle. Return to a full boil.
10. Process, following times given in individual recipes. Calculate from time water comes to a second boil. (Check with local extension agents for processing at high altitudes.)
11. Remove jars from canner and place on cloth-lined surface or wire rack at least 3 inches apart—*out of drafts*—until cool, about 12 hours.
12. Check seals. To test seal of closure with rubber ring, tip jar slightly. If jar is not properly sealed, bubbles start at the lid and rise through contents. For jars with two-piece vacuum lids, you must make certain a vacuum has been created. Usually you'll hear a slight pinging noise when this happens (as jars cool), but to make doubly sure, *press lid down in the center.*

If it does not push down at all, it is sealed. If it pushes down but then springs back up, the jar is not sealed. In this case, reprocess or refrigerate and eat immediately.

13. Remove metal rings from tightly sealed jars. Wipe jars with clean, dampened cloth; label, date and store in a cool, dark, dry place.

14. Check food for signs of spoilage before eating. Indications that food has spoiled include broken seals, seepage, mold, gassiness, spurting liquid when jar is opened, sliminess, cloudiness and unpleasant odors. *When in doubt, throw it out.*

### Preserving Tomatoes

1. About 3 pounds of fresh tomatoes are needed to fill a 1-quart jar. Wash plump, red, firm-ripe tomatoes in cool water; stem, then blanch 30 seconds. Quick-chill in cold water; core; remove any green spots and slip off the skins.

2. Drop whole tomatoes into clean, hot 1-quart canning jars (cut large tomatoes into quarters). Use a non-metallic kitchen utensil to press the tomato until the juice runs out. Add additional tomatoes, pressing out the juice until the jar is filled to within ½ inch of rim. If necessary, pour off a little juice or add tomato to achieve the proper head space. Add 1 sprig of fresh basil to each quart jar, if you wish. Add 1 teaspoon special canning salt to each quart jar (available at supermarkets).

3. Run a non-metallic utensil around edge of jars, between tomatoes and jar, to release any trapped air bubbles.

4. Wipe jar rims and seal jars. Process quarts in boiling water bath (212°) for 45 minutes.

5. Cool jars to room temperature, check seals, label and store on a cool, dark, dry shelf.

### Pickles and Relishes

Pickling includes any fruit or vegetable prepared by a pickling process, plus a wide variety of relishes.

There are two kinds of processing procedures:

*Brine cure:* Vegetables are held in a brine solution, about 4 to 6 weeks,

until fermentation takes place.

*Fresh-pack* or *quick-process:* Pickles are canned immediately after a brief simmer in a vinegar solution; some are soaked in a brine a few hours or overnight, and some call for treatment with ice water or boiling water before being covered with a pickling syrup. Relishes are prepared from chopped fruits and/or vegetables cooked in a spicy vinegar solution.

### Key to Successful Pickling

1. Use only fresh fruits and vegetables. Ideally they should be picked and used within 24 hours. Store in refrigerator without washing. Use unwaxed cucumbers only—brine will not penetrate wax. Foods should be the size needed for individual recipes.

2. Use pure granulated or canning salt. (The additives in table salt make the solution cloudy; iodized salt darkens pickles and retards fermentation.) Salt acts as a preservative and adds flavor and crispness to pickles. If you prefer kosher salt, use 1½ cups for every cup of fine granulated salt called for in the recipe.

3. Use only a high-grade cider or distilled white vinegar with an acid strength of 4% to 6% in pickling recipes.

4. Use only white granulated, cane or beet sugar unless the recipe calls for other kinds of sweeteners.

5. Use only fresh herbs and spices for a superior flavor.

6. Use soft water for making a pickling brine. (Hard water is not recommended because its minerals have a negative effect on the pickle. To soften hard water, boil 15 minutes. Let stand 24 hours. Skim off any film and ladle water into container without disturbing the sediment on the bottom. Add 1 tablespoon vinegar to each gallon boiled water.)

7. Do not use implements made of zinc, iron, brass, copper or galvanized metal. Also do not use cracked or chipped enamelware. For *fresh-pack method,* use unchipped enamelware, stainless steel or glass. For *fermenting or brining,* use a crock or stone jar, an unchipped enamel-lined pan, a bowl, casserole or large glass jar.

### SWEET PICKLE CHIPS

*Remember to keep these on hand for holiday gifts. They'll remind you of the pickles Grandma used to make.*

Makes 5 pints.

- **1 quart distilled white vinegar**
- **¾ cup sugar**
- **3 tablespoons canning salt**
- **2 teaspoons mustard seeds**
- **5 3-inch pieces stick cinnamon**
- **4 pounds small, firm cucumbers, sliced ¼-inch thick (12 cups)**
- **5 cups sugar**
- **2 cups distilled white vinegar**
- **1 tablespoon whole allspice**
- **2 teaspoons celery seeds**

1. Wash and rinse five 16-ounce jars and their closures. Keep jars and closures immersed in separate kettles of hot water until you are ready to use them.

2. Combine 1 quart vinegar, the ¾ cup sugar, canning salt, mustard seeds and stick cinnamon in a large, heavy, enamel or stainless steel kettle. Add cucumbers. Bring to boiling, stirring occasionally. Adjust heat; simmer 5 minutes; drain cucumbers; discard liquid but reserve cinnamon.

3. Combine remaining sugar and vinegar, allspice and celery seeds in kettle; bring to rolling boil over high heat.

4. Pack cucumbers into hot preserving jars, using a wide-mouth funnel, to within ¼ inch of tops; add 1 cinnamon stick to each jar. Pour hot liquid over pickles filling to ¼ inch of top, making sure there is enough syrup to cover pickles. Run a thin wooden or plastic spoon handle or other non-metallic utensil around edge of jars between food and jar to release any trapped air bubbles. Wipe jar rims and seal.

5. Process 10 minutes in a boiling water bath (212°). Remove jars from water bath; cool; check seals, then label and store on a cool, dark, dry shelf.

# Canning

## DILL PICKLES, KOSHER STYLE
Makes 6 quarts

- **30 to 36** Kirby cucumbers or other small cucumbers (3 to 4 inches long)
- **6** cups cider or distilled white vinegar
- **6** cups water
- **¾** cup canning salt
  Fresh or dried dillweed
  Garlic cloves, halved
  Mustard seeds

1. Wash and rinse six 32-ounce jars and their closures. Keep jars and closures immersed in separate kettles of hot water until you are ready to use.
2. Wash cucumbers thoroughly. Combine vinegar, water and salt in a kettle and bring to boiling.
3. Remove jars, one at a time, from water. Place a generous layer of dill, ½ to 1 clove garlic and 1½ teaspoons whole mustard seeds on bottom of each jar.
4. Pack cucumbers into jars. When the jars are half-filled, add more dill and complete the packing of the jars.
5. Pour hot brine over pickles, filling to ½ inch of top. Run a thin wooden or plastic spoon handle or other non-metallic utensil around edge of jars between food and jar to release any trapped air bubbles. Wipe jar rims and seal.
6. Process 20 minutes in boiling water bath (212°). Remove jars from water bath; cool. Pickles will shrivel after processing, but will plump in sealed jar. Check seals; label; store on a cool, dark, dry shelf.

— ●●● —

**CANTALOUPE** The origin of the cantaloupe is obscure. Its name comes from Cantalupo, a town near Rome, where the melon was planted in the 17th century from imported varieties. Now, the cantaloupe is cultivated in most warm regions of the world. Like its relative, the cucumber, the cantaloupe grows on long, trailing vines. Cantaloupe is in the muskmelon plant family along with casaba and honeydew.

Cantaloupe is delicious served as an appetizer with thinly sliced pros-ciutto (Italian-style ham) or as a dessert. See also **MELON**.

**Buying and Storing**: Choosing a ripe cantaloupe is no easy task. A ripe melon will have a distinct aroma and be somewhat springy when pressed lightly between your hands. Shaking the melon to hear the seeds slosh is *not* a good test for ripeness. Look for heavily netted skin and a smooth sunken scar at the stem end. Cantaloupe is in season from May to November, but can be found in some cities year-round. Plan to store cantaloupe 2 to 3 days at room temperature before serving. The flesh will soften and be juicier. Refrigerate the melon when ripe.

Plan on ¼ to ½ cantaloupe per serving. Half a 5-inch cantaloupe is an excellent source of vitamins A and C, with only 60 calories.

## COLD CANTALOUPE SOUP
*A chilly fruit combination to refresh the palate.*
Makes 4 cups.

- **1** ripe cantaloupe (about 2 pounds)
- **3** cups orange juice
- **½** teaspoon ground cinnamon
- **2** tablespoons lime juice
  Fresh mint sprigs

1. Pare, seed and cut melon into chunks. Place in container of electric blender with 1 cup of the orange juice; whirl until pureed.
2. Add remaining orange juice, cinnamon and lime juice; whirl 30 seconds.
3. Refrigerate thoroughly before serving. Just before serving; pour into bowls. Garnish with fresh mint.

## FROSTY CANTALOUPE COMPOTES
Makes 6 servings.

- **1** container (8 ounces) dairy sour cream
- **⅓** cup firmly packed light brown sugar
- **¼** teaspoon ground cinnamon
- **1** medium-size ripe cantaloupe
- **1** pint fresh blueberries, rinsed and drained
- **½** pound seedless green grapes, rinsed, drained and halved

1. Mix sour cream, brown sugar and cinnamon in a small bowl. Cover; chill until ready to serve.
2. Pare, seed and cut cantaloupe into 6 wedges; place each wedge in a serving bowl. Divide blueberries and grapes evenly among bowls; cover with plastic wrap; chill.
3. To serve: Spoon sour cream topping over fruit, dividing evenly.

— ●●● —

**CAPERS** The flower buds of a wild Mediterranean shrub which are salted and preserved in vinegar. They are used as a condiment or for seasoning sauce. Capers are sold in small bottles, usually imported from Spain, France or Italy. Refrigerate them once the bottle is opened; use to add a unique flavor to mayonnaise sauces and seafood or veal dishes.

## CHICKEN SALAD WITH CAPERS
Makes 4 servings.

- **2** whole chicken breasts (about 12 ounces each), cooked and chilled
- **½** cup chopped celery
- **2** tablespoons finely chopped onion
- **⅓** cup mayonnaise or salad dressing
- **1** tablespoon lemon juice
- **2** tablespoons drained capers
- **½** teaspoon salt
- **⅛** teaspoon pepper
  Lettuce leaves

1. Remove skin and bones from chicken breasts; cut meat into cubes (there should be about 3 cups).
2. Combine chicken, celery and onion in a medium-size bowl. Blend mayonnaise, lemon juice, capers, salt and pepper in a small bowl; add to chicken mixture. Toss well to coat. Serve on lettuce leaves.

— ●●● —

**CAPON** A male chicken, castrated while young so that it will grow plump and tender in a matter of months. A capon is marketed at 16 weeks of age and weighs from 4 to 7 pounds. It has a high proportion of white meat and a delicious flavor. It is excellent roasted, stewed or braised. See also **CHICKEN**.

**CARAMEL** This can either be a chewy candy or simply sugar that has been heated until it melts into a brown syrup. Caramel syrup is used to coat molds for custards or flans. Caramel candy is made of sugar, cream, butter and flavoring.

**CARAWAY** This fragrant herb, native to southeastern Europe and western Asia, has been used for thousands of years. Caraway is a biennial plant and a relative of the carrot. It has an edible fleshy yellowish-white root and small white flowers. After flowering, the seeds develop. Only the seeds are commercially available.

Caraway seeds are widely used in breads, rolls and biscuits, and provide the flavoring for the liqueur Kummel. Use caraway in coleslaw, sauerkraut dishes, potato salads, noodles or soups.

## CARAWAY KRAUT

Makes 4 servings.

  **5 bacon slices**
  **1 can (16 ounces) sauerkraut, drained**
  **1 can (16 ounces) stewed tomatoes**
  **1 teaspoon sugar**
  **½ teaspoon caraway seeds**
  **¼ teaspoon salt**
  **⅛ teaspoon pepper**

1. Cut 2 slices of the bacon into 1-inch pieces. Cook until crisp in a medium-size skillet; drain on paper toweling. Cook remaining 3 slices in same pan until almost crisp, then before removing from pan, roll each slice around the tines of a fork to make a curl; drain on paper toweling. Discard all drippings from pan.
2. Combine sauerkraut, tomatoes and liquid, sugar, caraway seeds, salt and pepper in the same skillet; heat to boiling; cover. Simmer 10 minutes.
3. Stir in bacon pieces; spoon into a heated serving bowl. Garnish with bacon curls and parsley, if you wish.

**CARDAMOM** The aromatic seed pods of the cardamom plant were first used in India for seasoning curries. The plant is a perennial that grows to a height of 8 feet, with 15 to 20 green stems bearing wide leaves. The flower stalks, on which the pods develop, grow from the base of the stem close to the ground.

Cardamom is commercially grown in India, Ceylon, Guatemala, Mexico and Thailand. It is available ground or as whole pods. The three-sided pods are creamy-white in color and are used to flavor hot fruit or wine punch, even coffee. Ground cardamom can be used in coffee cakes, rolls, pastries and cookies.

**CAROB** Often used as an alternative to chocolate, carob is sometimes called St. John's bread, locust seed or locust beans.

Carob is the fruit of an evergreen tree which grows along the shores of the eastern Mediterranean. The dark brown, flat pods are about 6 inches long, 1 to 2 inches wide. The pod is fleshy and sweet tasting, containing 4 to 12 hard brown seeds. Carob is harvested in the fall by farmers who shake the pods from the tree branches with long sticks. Then the pods are dried.

## HOT CAROB BUTTER FUDGE SAUCE

*Health food addicts claim many virtues for the fruit of the carob tree; at any rate, it makes a fine substitute for chocolate.*

Makes about 2¼ cups.

  **1 cup (2 sticks) butter or margarine, melted**
  **¾ cup honey**
  **¼ cup milk**
  **½ cup carob powder**
  **1 teaspoon instant coffee**

Combine butter, honey and milk in container of electric blender. Add carob powder and coffee slowly; whirl until smooth. Pour mixture into top of a double boiler, or a heavy medium-size saucepan. Place top over boiling water, or if using saucepan, simmer; lower heat. Cook, stirring constantly for 10 minutes. (Sauce burns easily, so watch carefully.) Serve over ice cream.

*Note:* Carob powder is sold in health food sections of supermarkets and in health food stores.

**CARP** This freshwater fish inhabits the muddy waters of many lakes, rivers and ponds throughout the world. First used for food in ancient China, the fish was introduced to America by German immigrants in 1876. Here, carp reproduced so quickly and in such great numbers, they literally took over many ponds and lakes, making the water uninhabitable for the local fish.

Although carp were never exceptionally popular in American cooking, they are a favorite in Chinese, central European and Jewish cooking. They can be stuffed and baked, broiled or deep-fried, smoked or pickled. The roe of carp is prized by some people.

In summer, a carp feeds on algae which gives its flesh a strong, muddy taste; for that reason, carp is better during the winter. It is relatively inexpensive and available in fish markets, usually whole, weighing 2 to 8 pounds.

**CARROT** A produce-counter staple, carrots are a thrifty and versatile vegetable. A plant with a pale yellow root was probably the predecessor of today's large, fleshy orange-rooted plant. It grew some 2,000 years ago in south central Asia and the Near East. Europeans found carrots easy to cultivate and nourishing. One carrot has only 20 calories and is an excellent source of vitamin A.

**Buying and Storing**: Many different varieties grown in many regions keep the supplies constant year-round. In most supermarkets, you'll find carrots with tops trimmed, washed and bagged in 1- or 3-pound sizes. Carrots sold with the tops intact have a shorter shelf life (they must be sold before the tops wilt or die), and so may be fresher than bagged carrots. They're also more expensive. Tiny fresh baby carrots, popular in Europe, are increasingly available in some markets. Cooked baby carrots are sold in cans or frozen.

# Carrot

Whichever type of carrots you buy, pick out well-shaped roots with smooth, clean skins. Store them in plastic bags in the refrigerator crisper. They will keep well for several weeks.

**To Prepare:** Carrots need only a good scraping or thin paring before washing, then they are ready for eating raw or for cooking. They can be cut into sticks, round or diagonal slices, diced or shredded. To make carrot flowers, see **GARNISHES**.

**To Cook:** Cooking time will depend on the size or cut of the carrots. Whole, sliced or diced carrots should be cooked in an inch of boiling water in a covered saucepan. Whole carrots will take about 15 minutes; slices or dices, about 10 minutes. Carrots baked with a roast will take about 45 minutes. To cook shredded carrots, combine carrots with 2 tablespoons water and butter or margarine. Cover and heat to boiling, then cook over low heat until tender.

**To Microwave:** Place 1 pound of whole carrots in a casserole with ½ cup water. Cover and microwave on high power 6 minutes. Rearrange carrots and microwave 6 more minutes or until tender. Let stand 2 minutes. For sliced carrots, reduce water to ¼ cup and microwave as above. For shredded carrots, do not add water; add 2 tablespoons butter. Cover and microwave 2 minutes. Stir carrots and microwave 1½ to 3 more minutes.

---

**Carrot Math**

1 pound fresh carrots = 4 servings or about 2½ cups cooked slices
1 pound fresh carrots = 3 to 4 cups shredded raw

---

## CARROT-PINEAPPLE CAKE

*Recipes for carrot cakes are popping up all over. Their popularity is well deserved, as they are moist, flavorful, and very good keepers.*

Bake at 350° for 1 hour, 15 minutes.
Makes one 10-inch tube cake.

- 4 eggs
- 1½ cups sugar
- 1½ cups vegetable oil
- 3¼ cups whole wheat flour
- 2 teaspoons baking powder
- 2 teaspoons baking soda
- ½ teaspoon salt
- 1 teaspoon ground cinnamon
- 1 can (8 ounces) crushed pineapple in pineapple juice, drained
- 2 cups shredded carrots
- 1 cup chopped pecans
- 1 cup chopped dates

1. Grease a 10-inch tube pan; line bottom with wax paper. Preheat oven to 350°.
2. Beat eggs in large mixing bowl. Gradually beat in sugar. Stir in oil.
3. Combine 3 cups of the whole wheat flour with baking powder, baking soda, salt and cinnamon. Stir into egg mixture. Add drained pineapple and carrots; mix well.
4. Toss pecans and dates with remaining ¼ cup whole wheat flour; stir into batter. Turn into prepared pan.
5. Bake in a preheated moderate oven (350°) for 1 hour, 15 minutes or until top of cake springs back when lightly pressed with fingertip. Cool cake in pan on wire rack about 15 minutes. Remove cake from pan; peel off wax paper. Cool completely before cutting. Wrap tightly in foil or plastic wrap to store. Cake keeps well.

## CARROT-STUFFED MUSHROOMS

Bake at 350° for 10 minutes.
Makes 8 servings.

- 8 large fresh mushrooms
- ¼ cup (½ stick) butter or margarine
- 1 tablespoon lemon juice
- 1 pound carrots, pared and sliced
- 2 tablespoons orange marmalade
- ¼ teaspoon ground ginger

1. Remove stems from mushrooms. (Reserve for another use.) Sauté mushrooms in butter and lemon juice until browned, about 3 minutes.
2. Cook carrots in boiling salted water until tender, about 8 minutes. Drain; stir in marmalade and ginger; puree in container of electric blender. Pipe puree through a pastry bag into mushroom caps. Place caps in a shallow baking dish.

3. Bake in a moderate oven (350°) for 10 minutes or until well heated.

## CARROTS LYONNAISE

*Cooking carrots this way brings out all their fresh, sweet taste.*

Makes 8 servings.

- ¼ cup (½ stick) butter or margarine
- 1 large onion, thinly sliced
- 2 pounds carrots, pared and cut into 2-inch sticks
- ¼ teaspoon salt
- ¾ teaspoon lemon pepper
- 2 tablespoons finely chopped fresh parsley

1. Melt 3 tablespoons of the butter or margarine in a skillet. Sauté onion until tender and golden. Remove from skillet with slotted spoon to a bowl; keep onion warm.
2. Add remaining tablespoon butter or margarine to same skillet. Toss carrots in skillet over medium heat to coat well with butter. Cover; lower heat. Cook 15 minutes or until carrots are tender. Uncover; continue to cook until liquid evaporates. Season carrots with salt, lemon pepper and parsley.
3. Lightly toss onion and carrots together; turn into heated serving dish.

## CARROT-RAISIN RELISH

*Serve this old favorite as is, or spoon into lettuce cups, salad style.*

Makes 6 servings.

- 3 cups shredded carrots
- 1 cup seedless raisins
- 1 tablespoon sugar
- 6 tablespoons mayonnaise or salad dressing
- 6 tablespoons light cream or half-and-half
- 1 tablespoon lemon juice
  Dash salt
  Dash pepper

1. Mix carrots and raisins in a bowl; sprinkle with sugar; toss lightly to mix. Chill at least 30 minutes.
2. Combine mayonnaise, cream, lemon juice, salt and pepper in a small bowl; stir into carrot mixture just before serving.

Pictured opposite: Carrots Lyonnaise, page 148

# Carrot

## MAPLE-BUTTER GLAZED CARROTS

*Maple syrup was the popular native-grown sweetener in the years before refined sugar.*

Makes 8 servings.

- 1 cup water
- 1 teaspoon salt
- 2 pounds carrots, pared, cut in half crosswise
- ¼ cup maple syrup
- ¼ cup (½ stick) butter or margarine
- 1 teaspoon leaf marjoram, crumbled
- 1 teaspoon salt
- ¼ teaspoon pepper

1. Bring water and 1 teaspoon salt to boiling in a medium-size heavy saucepan. Add carrots; return to boiling; cover. Simmer 15 minutes or until carrots are just tender. Drain thoroughly.

2. Cook maple syrup, butter, marjoram, salt and pepper in a large skillet over low heat 2 to 3 minutes or until bubbly and caramel-like in consistency.

3. Add carrots. Toss gently to coat in the maple butter. Cook over high heat, tossing gently, until carrots are glazed and liquid is absorbed.

———— •●● ————

**CARVING** Proper carving makes meat and poultry seem more tender. A good, razor-sharp knife does the cutting, but the hand that holds it must guide it properly. A good cutting board and some knowledge of the structure of the meat or bird are beneficial.

**Choosing Knives:** When buying a knife, remember the old saying "You get what you pay for." General-purpose, household knives can be purchased in supermarkets, discount stores or variety stores, but better quality knives are generally found in hardware, department or gourmet stores. Invest in good knives and they will last a lifetime. See **KNIVES.**

**Tips for Easier Carving:**
- Before carving a roast or poultry, let it stand 15 to 20 minutes.
- Use a two-pronged carving fork to hold the roast or bird securely.

# How to Carve Chicken or Turkey

To carve roast chicken or turkey, you need first of all a sharp, thin-blade knife and a sharp, long-tined fork. Keep your carving equipment in good condition and don't use them for any purpose other than carving.

Before you begin, be sure you remove from the bird all the trussing equipment—skewers, wooden picks, cord or thread.

Place the bird, breast up, on a serving platter or carving board large enough to make handling easy. You might have a separate plate nearby to hold drumsticks and wings out of the way as you remove them.

1. Place platter in front of you, the bird on its back with its legs toward your right. Grasping end of leg nearest you, bend it down toward platter while you cut through thigh joint to separate whole leg from body. Separate drumstick and thigh by cutting through joint.

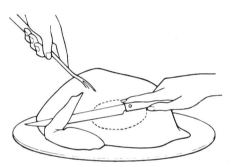

2. Stick fork into breast near breastbone and cut off wing close to body. Slanting knife inward slightly may make it easier for you to hit the joint.

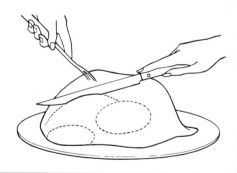

3. Slice white meat, starting at tip of breastbone and cutting down toward wing joint. Repeat with other side of bird, turning the platter if it is more convenient.

# How to Carve a Crown Roast of Veal, Lamb or Pork

Although it looks unusually showy, this is one of the easiest of all roasts to carve. Simply steady the roast on the platter with a fork, then use a sharp carving knife to cut down between the ribs, dividing the roast into chops. Serve each person one or two chops and, if the crown roast has been stuffed, a hearty spoonful of the stuffing.

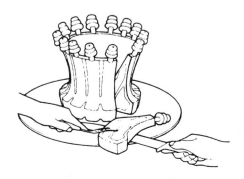

# How to Carve a Rolled Roast

**Beef:** If the shape of the roast permits, place broad-side down on platter and slice it horizontally, straight across the face of the meat, making the cuts as thick or thin as you like. The reason for this placement is to keep juices in the roast. However, if roast is long and narrow, it's best to put it on its side and carve straight down.

**Pork, veal and lamb roasts:** These are less juicy than beef roasts, and can rest on their sides. Simply carve straight down and through, from the top to the bottom.

# How to Carve a Whole Ham

Place the ham on platter with the decorated-fat-side up and shank bone to the carver's right (if he is right-handed; the reverse if he is left-handed).

Cut straight down through the boneless cushion in thin slices.

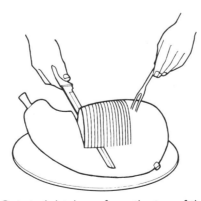

Cut straight down from the top of the ham to the leg bone in thin, even slices, then release slices by cutting along the bone.

# How to Carve a Shank Half of Ham

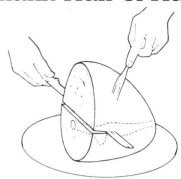

Place ham on platter with shank end at carver's left (the reverse if the carver is left-handed). The thick cushion side of the ham should be on top. Cut along leg bone and lift off chunky cushion.

Cut two or three slices off the thin side of the ham, which contains the kneecap.

To carve the shank portion containing the bone, cut around the leg bone with the tip of a carving knife to free meat from the bone. Turn meat so that thickest part is down, then slice straight down, making thin, even cuts.

# Carving

## How to Carve a Leg of Lamb

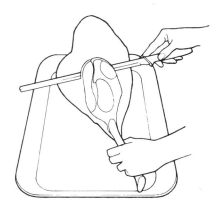

The French have the best—and the easiest—technique. Simply lift the leg bone with your hand, then slice down along (parallel to) the bone in thin slices.

## How to Carve a Standing Rib Roast

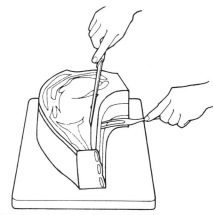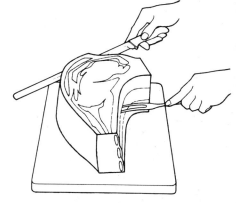

Place roast, broad-side down, on a large platter so that it stands firmly. Trim off any excess fat. Anchor roast with a fork; cut down along rib bones with a carving knife to free roast from the bones.

Slice straight across the broad side of the roast, making the slices as thick or thin as you like, cutting from the outer curved edge in to rib bones. The point of placing the roast on its broad side for carving, instead of standing it on its ribs, is that the juices will remain in the meat instead of running out on the platter.

---

**CASABA** The casaba is a large, round, smooth-skinned, light yellow to pale green melon. Its tough rind is marked with deep wrinkles longitudinally; its flesh is golden to creamy white.

Casaba, first cultivated in Persia, is in the same muskmelon family as cantaloupe and honeydew. It is available from July through November with the most plentiful supplies in September and October. One of the two most common varieties is the *golden,* which has an orange-yellow rind and golden flesh. The *pineapple* variety has a greenish-white rind and light yellow flesh.

A ripe melon will have a soft juicy flesh with no apparent aroma. A slight softening at the blossom end indicates ripeness. Keep casaba at room temperature until ripe, then refrigerate before serving.

To serve, cut in half and scoop out seeds. Cut melon into wedges or use a melon ball cutter to make melon balls. One melon, about 7 to 8 inches in diameter and weighing about 6 pounds, will make about 10 servings. A 2-inch wedge has only 38 calories.

**CASHEW** The cashew is native to Brazil. It was apparently carried by Portuguese explorers to India. Cashews are now imported from India to our markets and are also cultivated in many tropical areas of the Americas. The word cashew is derived from *caju,* a Portuguese adaptation of the original Brazilian Indian name of *acaju.*

The cashew tree is an evergreen that grows to a height of 36 feet. The nut is attached to the end of a fleshy, yellow-red stalk. The slightly tart stalks are eaten fresh by the people of South America, who call them cashew-apples or cashew-pears. The cashew nut is attached to the base of the cashew-apple. The pale beige, kidney-shaped nut is enclosed in a leathery shell, which has an acrid, irritating oil. For that reason, cashews are always shelled before they are sold. Most cashews are also roasted and salted before being sold, although raw cashews are becoming more available in local markets. One pound of cashews equals 3 to 3½ cups of kernels. For more information, see also **NUTS**.

### CASHEW-MUSHROOM STROGANOFF
Makes 4 servings.

- 1 **cup raw cashews or dry-roasted cashews**
- 4 **tablespoons butter**
- 1 **clove garlic, minced**
- 1 **medium-size onion, chopped**
- 1½ **pounds mushrooms, sliced**
- 3 **tablespoons whole wheat flour**
- 1 **tablespoon tomato paste**
- 1 **cup water**
- 3 **tablespoons tamari or soy sauce**
- 1 **cup dairy sour cream**
- 2 **tablespoons sherry**
  **Salt and pepper**

1. Place cashews in a 9-inch pie plate. Toast in a slow oven (250°) for 10 minutes or until lightly browned.
2. Melt 2 tablespoons of the butter in a large skillet. Sauté garlic, onion and mushrooms until soft but not brown, about 4 minutes. Remove to bowl with slotted spoon.
3. Add remaining 2 tablespoons butter to skillet. Stir in flour and tomato paste until smooth. Combine water with tamari; stir into tomato paste

---

mixture, stirring until well blended. Cook, stirring constantly, over medium heat until mixture thickens.
4. Stir in sour cream, sherry, mushrooms and cashews. Heat thoroughly, but do not boil. Taste; add additional salt and pepper, if needed. Garnish with chopped parsley, if you wish.

— • • • —

**CASSEROLE** A casserole is an inexpensive and convenient way to stretch your budget and pack a lot of nutrition into a main dish. But those bland and watery concoctions filled with indistinguishable ingredients have given this venerable dish a bad name.

Casseroles require only a salad and dessert to make a complete meal, which helps cut down on time and effort and simplifies serving and cleanup. Here are our tips on helping establish the casserole's popularity in your family.

**Preparation Pointers:**
● When a recipe calls for cooked meat or poultry, cook it ahead for easier slicing or cutting. If meat is cooked in broth, let it cool in the broth to retain juiciness and absorb flavor. Use broth and drippings in the casserole sauce.
● Cut food into attractive and identifiable sizes and shapes—generous cubes, strips or slices of meat, fish, poultry and diced or chopped vegetables.
● Cook rice or pasta for a casserole until barely tender, since it will get further cooking in the oven.
● Carefully follow recipe for sauce—a too-thick sauce will make a compact, gummy casserole; a too-thin sauce will be unattractive and runny.
● Instead of combining casserole ingredients with sauce, try layering them, then pouring sauce over the top. Ingredients stay identifiable, look pretty.
● Be sure to use the size casserole dish specified in the recipe.
● Bake at the temperature and for the time directed in recipe to prevent overcooking and drying. In general, a moderate oven temperature (350°) is

called for. Lower the temperature by 25° when using glassware or glass ceramic ware.

**Casserole Equipment**: Use casserole dishes that complement the food. There is a wide choice of sizes, shapes, colors and materials available. Glass ceramic dishes, for example, can go nonstop from refrigerator to freezer to oven. Others cannot adapt to these temperature extremes. So if you're preparing a casserole ahead, choose your dish accordingly.

You may want to freeze the mixture in a rigid plastic container, then transfer it to a casserole at baking time. Or, you can line a casserole with heavy-duty foil, allowing long overhanging ends, and fill with the cooked mixture. Then bring the ends of foil up over the mixture and fold together to seal firmly. (Be sure there are no leaks.) Place casserole in the freezer until food is frozen solid, then remove from casserole. Label the frozen packet and return it to the freezer. When you're ready to use it, unwrap and place it in the same casserole for reheating.

**CALIFORNIA CASSEROLE**
*A delicious, low-cost dish.*
Bake at 325° for 50 minutes.
Makes 6 servings.

    2 pounds zucchini and/or yellow squash
    1 large onion
    ¼ cup (½ stick) margarine
    2 tablespoons flour
    1 teaspoon dillweed
    1 teaspoon salt
    ¼ teaspoon pepper
    3 eggs
    1½ cups skim milk (made from dry milk powder)
    4 ounces Monterey Jack or Muenster cheese, shredded (1 cup)
    1 cup crushed cracker crumbs
    2 tablespoons margarine, melted

1. Trim squash and cut into thin slices; cut onion into slices and separate into rings. Preheat oven to 325°.
2. Sauté squash and onion in the ¼ cup margarine in a large skillet until soft; stir in flour, dillweed, salt and

pepper until well blended. Spoon into an 8-cup shallow casserole.
3. Beat eggs in a medium-size bowl; add milk; pour over vegetables; sprinkle cheese over.
4. Bake in a preheated slow oven (325°) for 40 minutes. Toss cracker crumbs with the 2 tablespoons melted margarine in a small bowl; sprinkle over casserole. Bake 10 minutes longer or until crumbs are golden and custard is set. Allow casserole to "rest" on a wire rack 10 minutes before serving.

**CHICKEN TORTILLA CASSEROLE**
Bake at 375° for 30 minutes.
Makes 6 to 8 servings.

    1 package (1 dozen) refrigerated or thawed frozen corn tortillas Vegetable oil
    2 cans condensed cream of chicken or mushroom soup
    ½ soup-can water
    1 can (4 ounces) diced, mild green chilies, drained (or use as much as you wish)
    3 cans (5 ounces each) chunk chicken, drained
    2 packages (4 ounces each) shredded Cheddar cheese (2 cups)
    1 jar (4 ounces) pimientos, drained and cut into slivers
    1 small head iceberg lettuce, shredded
    1 large onion, diced

1. Cook tortillas, 1 at a time, in ¼ inch hot oil in small skillet until just softened; drain on paper toweling.
2. Combine soup, water and chilies in a medium-size bowl. Preheat oven to 375°.
3. Layer ingredients in a 2-quart baking dish this way: Place 3 tortillas in bottom, overlapping to fit. Add 1 can of chicken, ½ cup cheese and some slivered pimiento, then top with ¼ of the soup mixture. Repeat layering 2 more times, ending with tortillas, soup mixture, then cheese. Cover with foil.
4. Bake in a preheated moderate oven (375°) for 30 minutes or until hot and bubbly. Cut into wedges. Serve with lettuce and onion.

# Casserole

## OVEN BEEF BURGUNDY

Bake at 350° for 1½ hours.
Makes 6 to 8 servings.

- **2** pounds beef round, cut into 1- to 1½-inch cubes
- **¼** cup all-purpose flour
- **1** teaspoon salt
- **¼** teaspoon pepper
- **2 to 4** tablespoons butter or margarine
- **2** tablespoons brandy
- **12 to 18** small white onions, peeled
- **½** pound medium-size mushrooms, halved
- **1** clove garlic, crushed
- **2** tablespoons chopped fresh parsley
- **¼** teaspoon leaf thyme, crumbled
- **1** cup condensed beef broth
- **1** cup red Burgundy wine
- **1** bay leaf

1. Shake meat with flour, salt and pepper in a plastic bag to coat well; reserve any remaining flour. Preheat oven to 350°.
2. Brown beef, about ¼ at a time, in hot butter in a large skillet or Dutch oven. Lift out beef as it browns and transfer to a 2½- or 3-quart casserole. Heat brandy in small saucepan; ignite and pour over beef. Add onions and mushrooms. Sprinkle in reserved seasoned flour over the beef and vegetables in casserole.
3. Stir garlic, parsley and thyme into drippings in skillet; cook 1 minute. Add beef broth and wine; heat, stirring to loosen browned bits, until mixture comes to boiling. Pour over beef and vegetables; add bay leaf. Cover.
4. Bake in a preheated moderate oven (350°) for 1 hour, 30 minutes or until meat is tender. Let casserole stand for 20 minutes before serving. Serve with white or wild rice mix, if you wish.

## GREEN RICE AND BACON CASSEROLE

Bake at 350° for 35 minutes.
Makes 6 servings.

- **1** medium-size onion, chopped (½ cup)
- **¼** cup (½ stick) butter or margarine
- **¼** cup all-purpose flour
- **1** teaspoon salt
- **⅛** teaspoon ground pepper
- **2½** cups milk
- **8** ounces Cheddar cheese, shredded (2 cups)
- **¼** cup chopped canned pimiento
- **1** package (10 ounces) frozen chopped spinach, thawed and well drained
- **3** cups cooked rice (¾ to 1 cup uncooked)
- **6 to 8** half-inch thick slices Canadian bacon (about 1¼ pounds)

1. Sauté onion in butter in a medium-size saucepan until golden brown. Blend in flour, salt and pepper. Add milk; cook over medium heat, stirring constantly, until sauce thickens and bubbles 1 minute. Add 1½ cups of the cheese and stir until melted. Stir in pimiento and spinach. Preheat oven to 350°.
2. Spoon half the rice into greased 2-quart casserole. Top with half the sauce. Repeat.
3. Overlap Canadian bacon on top, pressing one edge of each into rice mixture.
4. Bake in a preheated moderate oven (350°) for 30 minutes. Sprinkle remaining shredded cheese over top and bake 5 minutes longer or until cheese is melted and rice mixture is hot and bubbly.
*Note:* You can use 1¼ pounds cooked ham, sliced ½-inch thick, as a substitute for the Canadian bacon.

— ●●● —

**CASSOULET** A French stew made of dried white beans baked with meats, onions, garlic and herbs. There are many regional recipes. Some use preserved goose (*confit d'oie*), others use pork or lamb. Cassoulet ingredients were put into an earthenware dish called *cassolle d'Issel*, from which the name *cassoulet* is derived.

**CAULIFLOWER** A member of the Brassica or cabbage family. The most familiar are the creamy-white heads called "curd," but there are also green and purple varieties. Cauliflower is a good source of vitamins C and A, with 25 calories per 3½-ounce serving.

**Buying and Storing:** The best supplies are in the markets from September to November, but cauliflower is generally available year-round and is also sold frozen. Look for snowy, compact, heavy heads. One medium-size head, weighing about 1½ pounds, will make 4 servings.

Refrigerate cauliflower in its original wrapper or a plastic bag. Use within a few days.

**To Prepare:** Cut off the tough outer green leaves and cut the flowerets from the woody stem; wash well. Any tender green leaves can be cooked with the flowerets. The head of cauliflower can also be left whole, if you prefer.

**To Cook:** Add cauliflower to 1 inch of boiling water in a saucepan. Cover and cook a whole head about 20 minutes or flowerets 5 to 9 minutes. To preserve the whiteness, add some vinegar or lemon juice to the water. Do not overcook or it will become mushy and strong-flavored. Drain cauliflower and season with butter, buttered bread crumbs or a cheese sauce. If serving the cauliflower in a salad, rinse with cold water and chill quickly or marinate in a salad dressing in the refrigerator for at least one day before serving.

Flowerets are also delicious raw, in salads or on a vegetable platter with mayonnaise dip.

**To Microwave:** Wrap a whole 1-pound-size head with plastic wrap and place on a paper plate with the sealed edges down. Microwave on high power 3 minutes; turn cauliflower over and microwave 2½ to 4 more minutes or until the head is almost tender. Let stand 3 minutes to complete cooking. For flowerets, place in a casserole with ¼ cup water. Cover and microwave 3 minutes. Stir and microwave 1 to 2 more minutes. Let stand 2 minutes. Season with butter or herbs.

# Casserole

## CAULIFLOWER ITALIANO
Makes 8 servings.

**1 large cauliflower (about 3 pounds)**
**1 can condensed tomato bisque**
**1 package (8 ounces) mozzarella cheese, cut in strips**

1. Trim outer green leaves from cauliflower, but leave head whole. Cook, covered, in boiling salted water in a large saucepan 30 minutes or just until crisp-tender.
2. Lift out carefully; drain well. Place in a broiler-proof dish.
3. Heat tomato bisque to boiling in a small saucepan; spoon over cauliflower; top with cheese strips.
4. Broil 4 inches from heat, 5 minutes or just until cheese melts and starts to bubble. Or, bake in a hot oven (425°) for 10 minutes.

## CAULIFLOWER AND GREEN BEAN SALAD
Makes 6 servings.

**2 cups cooked cauliflower pieces**
**2 cups cooked cut green beans**
**½ cup diced canned pimiento**
**3 tablespoons olive or vegetable oil**
**2 tablespoons red wine vinegar**
**2 teaspoons salad seasoning with blue cheese**
**Salad greens**

1. Combine cauliflower and green beans in a bowl. Add pimiento.
2. Combine oil and vinegar in a small bowl or measuring cup; mix well. Pour over vegetables; sprinkle with salad seasoning. Toss well. Refrigerate 1 hour. Serve over salad greens.

● ● ●

**CELERIAC** Also called *celery root* or *celery knob,* this variety of celery is grown for its bulbous root rather than its spindly stalks and leaves. It is grown extensively in France, Italy and Germany. It is a turnip-shaped vegetable, about 2 to 4 inches in diameter, with a brownish, rough-textured skin. It may be eaten cooked or raw.

**Buying and Storing:** Celeriac is marketed from fall to spring. You can find it in produce markets or supermarkets of large cities catering to Euro-

pean cuisines. Select small to medium-size roots; large roots may be woody. Allow a half-pound per serving. Store in the refrigerator in a plastic bag; use within a week.

**To Prepare:** Scrub with a vegetable brush. Cut off any tops and root fibers. Celeriac will darken once it is pared, so drop it into a bowl of acidulated water. (Use about 3 tablespoons vinegar or lemon juice per quart of water.) Use pared small roots in salads or as a vegetable appetizer. Cut into julienne strips or coarsely shred and toss with French dressing or mayonnaise.

**To Cook:** Place pared, small roots in boiling water to cover and cook 20 minutes or until tender. Drain; serve with buttered, herbed bread crumbs or a cream sauce. Put pared slices in an inch of boiling water; cook 5 to 10 minutes or until tender; drain and season.

## CREAMED CELERIAC
Makes 6 servings.

**4 large celeriac (about 2 pounds)**
**2 tablespoons chopped onion**
**¼ cup (½ stick) butter or margarine**
**¼ cup all-purpose flour**
**½ teaspoon salt**
**¼ teaspoon dry mustard**
**Dash pepper**
**1 small can evaporated milk (⅔ cup)**

1. Pare celeriac and cut into thin slices. Cook in boiling lightly salted water in a medium-size saucepan 10 minutes or just until tender. (Celeriac darkens when cut, so cook it quickly.) Drain, reserving liquid in a 2-cup measure. Add water, if needed, to make 1⅓ cups.
2. While celeriac cooks, sauté onion lightly in butter in a medium-size saucepan. Stir in flour, salt, mustard and pepper; cook, stirring constantly, just until mixture bubbles.
3. Stir in reserved liquid, then evaporated milk. Continue cooking and stirring until sauce thickens and boils 1 minute. Stir in celeriac; heat just to boiling.

● ● ●

**CELERY** This versatile vegetable, found growing in southern Europe and Asia, was once considered a medicinal herb. Today's cultivated variety is totally edible with only 9 calories in a cup of raw slices. Italians are credited with serving celery as a table vegetable during the Middle Ages.

**Buying and Storing:** You'll find two varieties of celery in your markets all year: *Pascal,* or *green celery,* are the big plump bunches with thick crisp green stalks and perky green leaves. The other variety is called *Golden,* or *bleached celery.* These small, creamy-white bunches, known familiarly as hearts, are more expensive and have a mild, sweet flavor. Important buying guides for both are crispness, freshness and firm unbroken stalks.

Puzzled over which is right—stalk, bunch, rib or branch? Most recipes call for a measure of cut-up celery, so it doesn't really matter that much. However, it's interesting to note the difference between growers' terms and culinary terms. To a grower, the whole plant is a *stalk,* whereas we call it a *bunch.* Also, a *rib* or *branch* is what we call a *stalk.*

Celery that is sold in our markets is trimmed to about 12- to 16-inch-long bunches. A bunch of celery will make 4 to 6 servings. Celery hearts are shorter and smaller, so allow 1 celery heart for 2 servings.

Store celery as a bunch in the refrigerator vegetable crisper wrapped in a plastic bag. Celery will keep well up to a week.

**To Prepare:** Wash the celery. Snip off the leafy tops and wrap them to use for simmering with chicken or other meats. Dice or slice the outer stalks or cut into sticks. What's left is the tender heart to enjoy as a raw relish or an appetizer.

**To Cook:** Celery can be sautéed or stir-fried when sliced or cut into sticks. Celery hearts can be halved lengthwise and braised in chicken broth, then the cooking liquid can be thickened and used to sauce the hearts.

## CREAMED CELERY

Makes 6 servings.

- 4 cups sliced celery
- ¼ cup sliced green onions
- ¼ cup (½ stick) butter or margarine
- 2 tablespoons flour
- 1 cup canned chicken broth
- ⅛ teaspoon pepper
- ½ teaspoon Worcestershire sauce
- ½ cup light cream or half-and-half
- ¼ cup toasted slivered almonds

1. Sauté celery and onions in butter or margarine in a large skillet 10 minutes until crisp-tender.
2. Sprinkle flour over vegetables, blend in, then add chicken broth. Cook, stirring constantly, until the sauce thickens and bubbles 3 minutes. Stir in the pepper, Worcestershire sauce and cream and heat slowly, stirring, just until hot.
3. Spoon into a serving bowl; sprinkle with toasted slivered almonds.

## CELERY RELISH

Makes 4½ cups.

- 4 cups sliced celery
- 1 large onion, cut into sixths
- 1 jar (4 ounces) pimiento, drained
- 1 envelope unflavored gelatin
- 1 bottle (8 ounces) Italian salad dressing

1. Put celery, onion and pimiento into the container of an electric blender; reserve.
2. Mix gelatin and salad dressing in small saucepan. Stir over low heat just until gelatin is dissolved.
3. Pour gelatin mixture over vegetables in blender. Cover; whirl at low speed until ingredients are coarsely chopped.
4. Pour mixture into a bowl, cover and chill until thick. Serve as an accompaniment to hamburgers, frankfurters or fried fish. This relish keeps well for about a week.

— ••• —

**CELERY SEEDS** Although celery seeds taste like celery, they are harvested from a different plant which is related to parsley. The plant is grown extensively in France, India, Holland and also in the United States. Celery seed is available whole or ground. Use celery seeds in pickles, barbecue sauces, rolls or bread sticks. Celery salt is a combination of celery seeds and salt.

**CHAMPAGNE** Traditionally, only the sparkling wine from the Champagne district in northeastern France may be called champagne. But many wine-producing countries have sparkling wines termed champagne.

Almost all champagnes are white; a few are pink, but none are red. The best champagne is made by a special process in which the wine ferments for a second time in the bottle. This is largely responsible for the high price, since much hand labor is involved.

Champagne comes in various degrees of sweetness. *Brut* is very dry; *Extra dry* is dry but not quite as dry as Brut; *Demi-sec* is fairly sweet and *Sec* is sweet.

Champagne is an excellent all-purpose wine. It can be enjoyed before meals as a pre-dinner drink, during meals or with dessert. It must be served chilled but not icy.

French champagnes are best known, but California champagnes are excellent, too, and usually less expensive. New York also produces fine champagne.

Champagne is a blended wine, so if there is a vintage on the label, it only means that the wine was largely made from the wines produced in that single year. Vintage champagne will cost more than nonvintage champagne and have special appeal to connoisseurs.

How much champagne should you buy? It depends on the occasion and the number of guests you intend to serve. Generally speaking, figure on one bottle for every three guests. Most champagne comes in the new 750 milliliter-size bottle which is a little more than the former fifth size. It should provide four to six 4-ounce servings.

The bubbles in champagne come from natural carbonization. If the cork pops noisily, flies across the room and expensive champagne cascades onto your floor, you have opened the bottle incorrectly and lost some of the bubbles which have been developing. Hold the bottle with one hand and remove the wire muzzle with the other hand. Tilt the bottle away from you slightly and hold the cork firmly. Rotate the bottle and pull the bottle away from the cork. The cork should come out in your hand.

A tall tulip-shaped glass is best for champagne, rather than the shallow, saucer-shaped stemmed glasses. Too many bubbles are lost in the open glasses. After all, it's the bubbles that make drinking champagne fun! See also **WINE**.

## CHICKEN BREASTS IN CHAMPAGNE SAUCE

Makes 6 servings.

- 3 whole chicken breasts, split (2½ to 3 pounds)
- 3 tablespoons butter or margarine
- 1 teaspoon salt
- ¼ teaspoon pepper
- ½ teaspoon leaf thyme, crumbled
- ½ cup chicken broth
- 1½ cups dry champagne or dry white wine
- 2 tablespoons flour
- 2 egg yolks
- 1 package (6 ounces) long grain and wild rice mix, cooked following label directions

1. Brown chicken breasts in butter in a large skillet until golden brown, turning often (about 20 minutes).
2. Add salt, pepper, thyme, broth and 1¼ cups of the champagne to pan drippings in skillet. Bring to boiling; lower heat; cover. Simmer 20 minutes or until chicken is tender; remove chicken and keep warm.
3. Stir flour into remaining ¼ cup of champagne; stir mixture into liquid in skillet. Cook, stirring constantly, until mixture is thickened and bubbly.
4. Beat egg yolks in a small bowl; add about ½ cup of the hot sauce; stir back into skillet. Heat thoroughly, but do not boil.
5. To serve: Arrange chicken breasts on platter with hot rice; spoon a little sauce over each piece of chicken.

Overleaf: (From the top) Strawberry Cheesecake Deluxe, page 164; Chocolate Espresso Cheesecake, page 165; Cheddar and Beer Cheesecake, page 165

**ABZ's of Cooking 157**

# Champagne

**CHAMPAGNE PUNCH**

Makes about 30 four-ounce servings.

- ¼ **cup sugar**
- 1 **tablespoon aromatic bitters**
- ½ **cup fresh or frozen lemon juice**
- 1 **cup Cognac or brandy**
- 1 **cup orange-flavored liqueur**
- 2 **bottles (750 ml. each) dry champagne, chilled**
- 2 **bottles (28 ounces each) club soda, chilled**
- 1 **large block ice\***
  **Lemon and orange slices**

1. Combine sugar, bitters and lemon juice in large punch bowl; stir to dissolve sugar. Add Cognac and liqueur.
2. Just before serving, pour in champagne and club soda; stir to blend. Add block of ice, lemon and orange slices.

*To make ice block: A day or so ahead of time, fill a 1½-quart bowl or decorative mold with cold water; place in freezer until frozen solid. To unmold, run cold water over mold to loosen; slide ice block into punch.*

———— •●• ————

**CHARCOAL COOKING** See **BAR-BECUE.**

**CHARD** See **SWISS CHARD.**

**CHEDDAR** More Cheddar is consumed annually in this country than any other type of cheese. Cheddar is named after a small village in Somerset, England, where the cheese was first made in the 17th century. The best Cheddars were farm-made, aged from 2 to 5 years to develop a firm, sharp taste with a natural, pale gold color. Factory-made Cheddar cheese is an American innovation.

Today, Cheddar cheese is made in many parts of the world, including Canada, Australia, New Zealand and France. American-made Cheddars are usually named for the state or county of origin. Vermont, New York, and Wisconsin are big Cheddar cheese producers. Colby, named after a Wisconsin town, is a type of Cheddar which contains less salt and is marketed within four weeks after manufacturing. Longhorn is a mild Cheddar named after a breed of cow

## A QUICK TABLE OF

| KIND | DESCRIPTION | FLAVOR | USES |
|---|---|---|---|
| **American** | Process cheese of uniform texture made from domestic Cheddar; comes in slices and loaves. | Mild. Very popular with children. | A favorite for sandwiches and casseroles |
| **Bel Paese** | Mellow, semi-soft Italian cheese. | Mildly nutty. | Superb teamed with fresh fruit as dessert. Also good with cocktails. |
| **Blue, Gorgonzola, Roquefort, Stilton** | Medium-soft with blue to blue-green veins, crumbles easily. | Mild to tangy, slightly peppery. | These give a gourmet touch to appetizers, salads, dressings, desserts. |
| **Brie, Camembert** | Rounds and wedges with an edible gray-white crust; soft inside. | Mild to pungent, depending on age. | Favorites for desserts and appetizers. Serve at room temperature. |
| **Cheddar** | Semi-hard, cream to orange color. Sold as wedges, blocks, cubes, slices; also shredded. | Mild to very sharp, depending on aging. Always clearly marked on the package. | America's choice for sandwiches, cooked dishes, salads, snacks, desserts. |
| **Cottage, Ricotta, Cream** | Cottage and ricotta are creamy-white curd-like, low-calorie. Cream cheese is smooth and calorie-rich. | All are delicately mild; easily spoonable and spreadable. | Perfect for appetizers, sandwiches, cooked dishes, desserts, cake fillings or frostings. |
| **Edam, Gouda** | Creamy orange with red-wax coat. Edam is round; Gouda, flattish. | Mellow, slightly salty, with a nut-like taste. | Excellent for appetizer and dessert trays. Good snack cheeses, too. |

## POPULAR CHEESES

| KIND | DESCRIPTION | FLAVOR | USES |
|---|---|---|---|
| **Gruyère** | Smooth, firm, pale, cream-colored cheese; process Gruyère is often sold in foil-wrapped triangles. | Nut-like, faintly caramel. | An all-purpose cheese, excellent for sauces, toppings. Also good in salads, soufflés and omelets. Delicious eaten out-of-hand. |
| **Liederkranz, Limburger** | Soft, bacteria-ripened cheese. | Strong to overpowering; acquired tastes. | Best eaten out-of-hand or on crackers. |
| **Mozzarella** | Soft and white with a ball-like shape. Also comes shredded. | Mild and a bit chewy to eat, especially when heated. | Known as the pizza-lasagna cheese. Use in salads or on appetizer platters. |
| **Muenster, Brick** | Creamy-yellow to white; semi-soft; tiny holes. | Muenster is mild; Brick, mild to sharp. | Appetizers, sandwiches, salads, desserts. |
| **Parmesan, Romano, Sapsago** | The grating cheeses—very hard. White to light green. Sold in blocks, as well as grated. | Parmesan is pungent, but milder than Romano. Sapsago has herb-like flavor. | Topper for casserole dishes and spaghetti. Also popular for sauces and vegetable seasoners. |
| **Port du Salut** | Firm, smooth French cheese, the color of cream. | Fairly sharp. | A good cocktail or dessert cheese. |
| **Provolone** | Light brown outside; light yellow inside. Sometimes lined with rope marks. | Mellow to sharp, smoky and salty. | Try it in macaroni, spaghetti dishes, for sandwiches, snacks or appetizer trays. |
| **Swiss** | Light to creamy-yellow; large uneven holes. Buy sliced or in cuts. | Mild, with nut-like sweetness. One of our most popular cheeses. | Same as Cheddar, but in cooked dishes it may string somewhat. |

from whose milk the cheese was originally made. Tillamook is made in the Oregon county of that name.

Cheddar cheese is not always orange-colored. A true Cheddar may be off-white in color. Most Cheddar is tinted with annatto, a natural yellowish-red vegetable dye from the seeds of a tropical tree. In olden days, marigold petals or coloring from carrots were used to tint cheese curds. For more information, see **CHEESE**.

**CHEESE** There are literally hundreds of different kinds of cheeses in the world, yet all have the same main ingredient—milk. Milk is curdled by the action of heat or rennet (or other bacteria) or both, then the watery part, called whey, is separated from the curd. The curd, sometimes the whey, is made into cheese.

The origin of cheese-making is lost in antiquity. It was probably discovered by chance. Records show that cheese was known to the Sumerians in 4000 B.C. We do know that cheese existed in Biblical times. Roman conquerors probably introduced cheese to England. Cheese was made by monks during the Middle Ages.

The word "cheese" comes from *cese* or *cyse* in Old English. To the French, cheese is *fromage;* Italians call it *fromaggio.*

Cheese-making begins with milk, usually cow's milk. Goat's or ewe's (sheep) milk is also used in making some cheese. Cow's milk can be whole, skimmed or with more cream added. Milk may be sweet or sour; or cow's milk may be mixed with other types of milk. Cheese differs according to the milk used and the manufacturing process. The method used to curdle milk, what flavors or organisms are added and how the cheese is ripened and aged all give cheeses their distinct characteristics.

Cheese is divided into two categories. The first is *natural cheeses.* The other category is *cheese blends,* in which natural cheeses are used to make new products.

*Natural cheeses* may be subdivided by texture or consistency and

# Cheese

degree or kind of ripening. The amount of whey drained from the curd generally determines the consistency of the cheese. Examples:

- Very hard—Parmesan, Romano
- Hard—Cheddar, Swiss
- Semi-soft to hard—Colby, Gouda
- Semi-soft—Blue, Brick, Muenster, Roquefort
- Soft—Brie, Camembert, cottage cheese, cream cheese, Limburger, Neufchâtel, ricotta.

*Cheese blends* can be subdivided into three products:

- Pasteurized process cheese is a blend of shredded fresh and aged natural cheeses heated with water and an emulsifier to an homogeneous mixture. It is shaped into loaves or wheels. Buy it by the piece, or presliced or cut up and packaged. Popular-priced, it is perfect for cooking or making sandwiches. American cheese is an example.
- Pasteurized process cheese food is made the same way as process cheese, but with nonfat dry milk added. The moisture content is higher so it is softer and spreads more easily. It will melt faster than process cheese. It is packaged as loaves, rolls or links.
- Pasteurized process cheese spread is similar to process cheese food but spreads more easily because it contains more moisture. The milk fat content is lower. It's packaged in jars, tubes and pressurized cans. Some may be flavored with pimiento, olives or onions. Cheese spreads can be used for appetizers and sandwiches.

**Buying Cheese:** Remember that cheese is perishable. Buy often and only what you can use in a short time. Larger pieces or packages are usually your thriftiest buys. Aged cheese is highest in price; save the aged cheeses for the cheese board. For cooking, use less costly, "younger" cheeses which may be labeled mild. An aged cheese may be labeled sharp.

**Storing Cheese:** The softer the cheese, the more perishable it is. The harder the cheese, the longer it will keep. Keep cheese chilled, the same

as milk. Use soft cheese—cottage, cream, ricotta, Brie—within a week. Hard cheeses will keep for weeks if left in their original wrapper or re-wrapped tightly with plastic wrap. Should the surface of a hard cheese get moldy, simply cut off the affected area. Cheese mold is harmless and should not affect the cheese's quality. Some pasteurized cheese products do not need refrigeration, but once they are opened, they should be refrigerated if labels direct. Freeze cheese only if you must. Cheese loses flavor and becomes crumbly when frozen.

**Cooking Cheese:** Cheese is very heat sensitive and can curdle or become rubbery with excessive heat. Cook cheese over low or moderate heat. Since it melts quickly, you really don't need much heat. When making a cheese sauce, add the cheese last and cook just to melt it.

**Cheese Nutrition:** Cheese is a good source of high-quality protein (as that in meat, poultry and eggs). It contains most of the nutrients of milk, including calcium and riboflavin.

For more information on cheeses, see specific cheeses such as **BLUE, BRICK, BRIE, CAMEMBERT, CHEDDAR, COTTAGE CHEESE, LIEDERKRANZ.**

---

### Cheese Math

1 pound hard cheese (Cheddar, Swiss) = 4 cups shredded
1 pound hard, semi-soft or soft cheese = 4 servings
1 pound cottage cheese = 2 cups

---

## ALL-AMERICAN MACARONI AND CHEESE

Bake at 350° for 30 minutes.
Makes 4 servings.

- 1½ cups elbow macaroni, rigati or ziti
- ¼ cup (½ stick) butter or margarine
- 1 cup fresh bread crumbs (2 slices)
- 1 large zucchini, sliced
- 1 small onion, chopped (¼ cup)
- 3 tablespoons flour
- 2½ cups milk

- 2 tablespoons prepared mustard
- 1 teaspoon Worcestershire sauce
- 6 ounces process American cheese
- 1 large tomato

1. Cook pasta in boiling salted water, following label directions.
2. While pasta cooks, melt margarine in a medium-size saucepan; toss 1 tablespoon with bread crumbs in a small bowl and reserve.
3. Sauté zucchini slices in margarine in saucepan 2 minutes; remove with slotted spoon and reserve. Sauté onion until soft in margarine; stir in flour and cook 1 minute; remove from heat. Gradually stir in milk until smooth. Cook, stirring constantly, 3 minutes; stir in prepared mustard and Worcestershire sauce.
4. Shred 1 cup of the cheese (about 4 ounces) and stir into saucepan until melted; drain pasta and return to kettle; pour sauce over and blend well; pour into an 8-cup shallow casserole.
5. Cut tomato into wedges; make a pretty pattern on macaroni using the zucchini slices, tomato wedges and buttered crumbs; cut remaining cheese into thin slices; place on casserole.
6. Bake in moderate oven (350°) for 30 minutes or until crumbs are golden and casserole is bubbling-hot.

## CHEESE PUFFS

Bake at 350° for 15 minutes.
Makes about 4 dozen.

- ½ cup (1 stick) butter or margarine, softened
- 8 ounces process American cheese, shredded
- 1 cup *unsifted* all-purpose flour
- ¼ teaspoon salt

1. Preheat oven to 350°. Beat butter and cheese in a medium-size bowl with electric mixer until smooth. Stir in flour and salt until well mixed; knead lightly with hands to form a soft dough.
2. Roll into balls, 1 teaspoon at a time; place on greased cookie sheets.
3. Bake in a preheated moderate oven (350°) for 15 minutes or until golden. Serve hot.

Pictured opposite: Champagne Punch, page 160

# Cheese

## NEVER-FAIL CHEESE SOUFFLÉ

Bake at 400°, then at 375° for 30 minutes.
Makes 4 servings.

- 2 ounces Swiss cheese, shredded (½ cup)
- 6 tablespoons freshly grated Parmesan cheese
- 1 tablespoon butter or margarine
- 5 eggs
- 2 tablespoons butter or margarine
- 2 tablespoons flour
- ½ teaspoon salt
  Pinch cayenne
  Pinch ground nutmeg
- 1 cup skim milk or liquified non-fat dry milk
- ¼ teaspoon cream of tartar

1. Combine the Swiss cheese with 4 tablespoons of the Parmesan in a small bowl; reserve. Butter a 2-quart soufflé dish or other straight-sided dish with the 1 tablespoon butter. Sprinkle the remaining 2 tablespoons Parmesan over buttered surface to coat. Preheat oven to 400°.
2. Separate 4 of the eggs, putting the yolks into a cup and the whites in a large bowl. Separate the fifth egg, putting the white with the other whites. Refrigerate the yolk for another use.
3. Melt remaining 2 tablespoons butter in a medium-size saucepan. Add flour, salt, cayenne and nutmeg; cook and stir 1 minute; stir in milk. Cook, stirring constantly, until thickened and bubbly, about 3 minutes. Remove from heat; stir in yolks, 1 at a time, until mixture is smooth. Stir in cheese mixture.
4. Beat whites with cream of tartar in a large bowl with electric mixer until soft peaks form. Stir ¼ of the beaten whites into the cheese sauce to lighten; gently fold in remaining whites. Turn into prepared dish. Scoop a trough around the mixture about an inch in from the edge to give a "high hat" effect. Place soufflé in center of preheated oven; lower heat to moderate (375°).
5. Bake for 30 minutes or until soufflé is risen and nicely browned.

— ●●● —

**CHEESECAKE** Who can resist a luscious strawberry-topped cheesecake? This dessert rivals apple pie in popularity and has become a standard dessert on restaurant menus. More cheesecake is consumed in this country than anywhere else. Today you can find everything from tofu cheesecakes to "no cheese" cheesecakes.

Just about every country that produces cheese has a sweet cheese dessert similar to cheesecake. Some are made like custard pies, some are chilled and molded in a special shape. Italy's *Torta di Ricotta* and *Cassata alla Siciliana* are popular cheese desserts. Greece has *melopita,* a honey-sweetened cheese mixture in pastry. No matter where a cheesecake is made, its basis is usually a fresh, soft, unripened cheese like cream cheese, ricotta, cottage or pot cheese.

## STRAWBERRY CHEESECAKE DELUXE

Bake at 475° for 12 minutes, then at 250° for 1½ hours.
Makes 16 to 20 servings.

- 5 packages (8 ounces each) cream cheese
  Sweet Pastry (recipe follows)
- 1¾ cups sugar
- 3 tablespoons flour
- 5 eggs
- 2 egg yolks
- 1 tablespoon grated lemon rind
- ¼ cup heavy cream
  Strawberry Topping (recipe follows)

1. Let the cream cheese soften to room temperature in a large bowl while preparing the Sweet Pastry. Preheat oven to 400°.
2. Roll ⅓ of chilled Sweet Pastry between two pieces of wax paper to a circle 9 inches in diameter. Remove top sheet of wax paper. Invert dough onto bottom of a 9-inch springform pan. Carefully remove remaining wax paper. Press dough to fit inside rim.
3. Bake in a preheated hot oven (400°) for 6 minutes or until lightly browned; cool. Butter side of springform pan; fit over cooled bottom. Roll remaining dough into a rectangle, 4 inches wide and 15 inches long, between two pieces of wax paper; remove top sheet of wax paper and cut dough in half lengthwise through bottom paper; press on side of pan; remove remaining wax paper; press firmly to bottom. Refrigerate. Raise oven temperature to 475°.
4. Beat cheese with electric mixer at medium speed just until smooth. Add sugar gradually, beating just until light and fluffy; sprinkle flour over mixture; blend thoroughly. Add eggs and egg yolks, one at a time, beating well after each addition. Beat in lemon rind and heavy cream on *low* speed. Pour into prepared pan.
5. Bake in a preheated very hot oven (475°) for 12 minutes; lower temperature to 250° and bake 1½ hours. Turn off oven heat and let cake remain in oven, with door ajar, 30 minutes longer.
6. Remove cake from oven; let cake cool completely on wire rack.
7. Decorate top with Strawberry Topping. Refrigerate several hours or overnight.
8. To serve: Loosen cake around edge with metal spatula; then remove side of springform pan. Serve at room temperature. Keep leftover cake in refrigerator.

**Sweet Pastry:** Combine 1 cup *sifted* all-purpose flour with ¼ cup sugar in a medium-size bowl; cut in 6 tablespoons butter with knife or pastry blender until mixture is crumbly. Add 1 egg yolk, slightly beaten, and ½ teaspoon vanilla; mix lightly with fork just until pastry is moistened; shape into ball with fingers. Wrap in wax paper; chill 1 hour.

**Strawberry Topping:** Wash, pat dry and hull 4 cups (2 pints) strawberries. Combine ½ cup red currant jelly and 1 tablespoon sugar in a small saucepan; bring to boiling over low heat, stirring constantly; boil 1 minute; remove from heat; cool slightly. Dip strawberries into jelly to coat. Transfer to wax paper-lined wire rack with stem-side down; let set. When glaze has set, arrange strawberries on top of cheesecake.

# Cherries

## CHOCOLATE ESPRESSO CHEESECAKE

Bake at 350° for 1 hour.
Makes 16 to 20 servings.

- 3 packages (8 ounces each) cream cheese
- 26 packaged chocolate wafers, crushed (1½ cups)
- 2 tablespoons sugar
- ¼ cup (½ stick) butter or margarine, melted
- 1 package (12 ounces) semisweet chocolate pieces
- 2 tablespoons instant espresso coffee
- 2 tablespoons hot water
- 1 cup sugar
- 3 tablespoons flour
- 3 eggs
- 2 egg yolks
- 1 cup heavy cream

1. Let the cream cheese soften to room temperature in a large bowl.
2. Blend crumbs, 2 tablespoons sugar and butter in a medium-size bowl. Press firmly over the bottom and halfway up the side of a lightly buttered 9-inch springform pan. Chill before filling. Preheat oven to 350°.
3. Melt chocolate in top of double boiler over hot, not boiling, water. Dissolve espresso in 2 tablespoons hot water.
4. Beat cream cheese with electric mixer at medium speed just until smooth. Add 1 cup sugar gradually, beating just until light and fluffy; sprinkle flour over mixture; blend thoroughly. Add eggs and egg yolks, one at a time; beat well after each.
5. Beat in melted chocolate, dissolved espresso and cream at *low* speed. Pour into prepared pan.
6. Bake in a preheated moderate oven (350°) for 1 hour. Turn off oven heat and let cake remain in oven, with door closed, 40 minutes longer.
7. Remove cake from oven; let cake cool completely on wire rack. Refrigerate several hours or overnight.
8. To serve: Loosen cake around edge with metal spatula; remove side of springform pan. Serve at room temperature, but keep leftover cake in refrigerator. Garnish with whipped cream rosettes and chocolate curls, if you wish.

## CHEDDAR AND BEER CHEESECAKE

Bake at 300° for 2 hours.
Makes 16 to 20 servings.

- 4 packages (8 ounces each) cream cheese
- 6 ounces extra sharp Cheddar cheese, finely shredded (1½ cups)
- 1 box (6 ounces) zwieback crackers, crushed (1½ cups)
- ¼ cup sugar
- ¼ cup (½ stick) butter or margarine, melted
- 1¾ cups sugar
- 4 eggs
- 2 egg yolks
- ⅓ cup beer
- ¼ cup heavy cream

1. Let the cream cheese and grated Cheddar soften to room temperature in a large bowl. Preheat oven to 300°.
2. Combine zwieback crumbs, ¼ cup sugar and butter in a medium-size bowl. Press firmly over the bottom and halfway up the side of a lightly buttered 9-inch springform pan. Chill briefly before filling.
3. Beat cheeses with electric mixer at medium speed just until smooth. Add 1¾ cups sugar gradually, beating just until light and fluffy. Add eggs and egg yolks, one at a time, beating well after each addition. Beat in beer and heavy cream at *low* speed. Pour into prepared pan.
4. Bake in a preheated slow oven (300°) for 2 hours. Turn off oven heat and let cake remain in oven, with door ajar, 30 minutes longer.
5. Remove cake from oven; let cool completely on wire rack. Refrigerate several hours or overnight.
6. To serve: Loosen cake around edge with metal spatula; remove side of springform pan. Serve at room temperature, but keep leftover cake in refrigerator. Garnish with frosted green grapes, if you wish.
**To Frost Grapes**: Dip small clusters of green grapes in slightly beaten egg white; sprinkle with granulated sugar. Let dry on wire rack.

—————— ●●● ——————

**CHERRIES** The numerous varieties of cherries can be divided into two groups: sweet and sour. Sweet cherries include Bing, a large, heart-shaped deep red to purple cherry, and Royal Ann, which has a light gold skin with a pink blush. Sour cherries are red, roundish and smaller than sweet cherries.

The cherry is a member of the rose family. The trees are probably native to western Asia, where wild varieties grow. From there, cherry cultivation spread westward. Cherries were grown in Egypt about 600 B.C., and cherry pits were found in ancient Swiss and Italian dwellings.

**Buying and Storing**: During their short summer season, from May to July, fresh sweet cherries are a treat. Some are canned in syrup or frozen in bags. Sour cherries are also found fresh for a brief time during the summer; most are canned in water or made into pie filling and preserves, or candied as red or green cherries. Many states produce some cherries, but sweet cherries are grown mainly in Washington, Oregon, California and New York. Sour cherries come from Michigan, New York, Pennsylvania and Wisconsin.

Maraschino cherries are made from sweet light-colored cherries. They are bleached, pitted and steeped in a colored sugar syrup. Maraschino cherries here are unlike their European predecessors. Italians soak white, sweet cherries in a cherry liqueur called *maraschino*, made from the marasca cherry. The French also soak some cherries in a sugar syrup and call them maraschino. Americans have developed their own recipe for making maraschino cherries based on European techniques.

Cherries are very important in the liquor industry. Besides maraschino liqueur, there is kirsch, a cherry brandy made by fermenting the cherry pulp with crushed pits. The liquid obtained is distilled several times to obtain a clear brandy with a 40% to 50% alcohol content. Kirsch is used in desserts and cheese fondues.

When buying fresh cherries, look

# Cherries

for firm, brightly-colored fruit that does not feel sticky. Cherries are delicate and perishable, so use within a few days. One pound fresh cherries will give you about 2 cups pitted. Allow ¼ pound per serving.

## CLAFOUTI

*Traditionally made with just-picked, unpitted cherries (the seeds contain the perfume, according to the French), clafouti is just as good baked with peach wedges or apricot halves.*

Bake at 400° for 45 minutes.
Makes 6 servings.

- **1 pound fresh sweet cherries, OR 1 can (17 ounces) dark sweet cherries**
- **½ cup *sifted* unbleached all-purpose flour**
- **⅔ cup sugar**
  **Pinch salt**
- **3 eggs, slightly beaten**
- **1½ cups milk**
- **3 tablespoons butter or margarine, melted and cooled**

1. Wash and dry fresh cherries, or thoroughly drain canned cherries. Preheat oven to 400°.
2. In a large bowl, combine flour, ½ cup of the sugar and salt. Add eggs, blending thoroughly with a wire whisk or wooden spoon. Add milk and melted butter, stirring until mixture is quite smooth. (Do not beat.)
3. Butter a 9 × 9 × 2-inch baking pan. Sprinkle in 1 tablespoon of the remaining sugar. Spread cherries on bottom; pour into batter.
4. Bake in a preheated hot oven (400°) for 30 minutes. Sprinkle top with remaining sugar. Continue baking for 15 minutes or until the custard is firm and a knife inserted near center comes out clean.

## INSTANT CHERRY CRISP

Bake at 350° for 10 to 15 minutes.
Makes 8 servings.

- **2½ cups ready-to-eat granola-type cereal with raisins and dates**
- **1 can (21 ounces) cherry pie filling**
- **2 tablespoons butter or margarine**

1. Preheat oven to 350°. Sprinkle 1 cup of the cereal in an 8 × 8 × 2-inch baking dish; spoon pie filling over, then sprinkle remaining cereal over top; press down slightly into filling. Dot with butter.
2. Bake in a preheated moderate oven (350°) for 10 to 15 minutes or just until heated through. Serve with softened vanilla ice cream, if you wish.

## FRESH CHERRY PIE

Bake at 425° for 45 minutes.
Makes one 9-inch pie with lattice crust.

- **1 package (11 ounces) piecrust mix**
- **½ cup ground blanched almonds**
- **4 cups pitted fresh sour cherries OR: 2 cans (16 ounces each) pitted sour red cherries, drained**
- **1¼ cups sugar**
- **2 tablespoons quick-cooking tapioca**
- **¼ teaspoon salt**

1. Combine piecrust mix with almonds in a medium-size bowl; prepare piecrust mix following label directions.
2. Mix cherries, sugar, tapioca and salt in a medium-size bowl. Toss lightly to coat fruit; let stand 20 minutes.
3. Roll out half of pastry to a 12-inch round on a lightly floured surface; fit into a 9-inch pie plate; trim overhang to ½ inch. Spoon cherry mixture into prepared pastry shell. Preheat oven to 425°.
4. Roll out remaining pastry to an 11-inch round. Cut in ½-inch strips with a pastry wheel or knife. Weave strips into lattice over filling. Turn ends under; flute. Tear off 2-inch piece of aluminum foil; crumple lightly over fluted edge to keep edge from over-browning.
5. Bake in a preheated hot oven (425°) for 30 minutes; remove foil; continue baking 15 minutes or until pastry is brown and filling bubbly. Serve warm with vanilla ice cream, if you wish.

● ● ●

**CHERVIL** This herb, a relative of parsley, has lace-like leaves with a slight anise taste. It is most popular in French cuisine—in salads and the classic combination of *fines herbes.* Its origin is vague; likely from southeastern Europe or western Asia.

Chervil is easily grown from seed, and will reseed itself each year if the flowers are allowed to mature. It is readily available dried. Try a pinch in egg or seafood dishes; fresh leaves are delicious in salads.

**CHESTNUT** A fall-to-winter holiday treat, chestnuts were once abundant in the Northeast; trees grew as far south as Alabama. American chestnut trees were destroyed by a blight in the early 1900's. Today most of the chestnuts on the market, whether fresh, canned or dried, are imported, with some limited amounts being grown in California.

The meat of the chestnut is actually a seed covered by a leathery brown shell. On the tree, 1 to 3 chestnuts are encased in a round, prickly hull.

Southern Europeans are great chestnut fans and use them as a staple food—ground into flour, eaten fresh as a vegetable or sweetened for desserts. The Chinese use a variety of chestnuts in stir-fried dishes and add them to soups or stuff them into rice dumplings. (These Chinese chestnuts are similar to the European chestnuts and should not be confused with water chestnuts. For more information, see **WATER CHESTNUT.**) Japanese chestnuts are smaller and less sweet than the Chinese or European nuts.

Chestnuts may be served not only as a snack but also added to stuffing or mixed with green vegetables. When sweetened, they make rich desserts.

**Buying and Storing:** Imported from Italy or Spain, fresh chestnuts are found from October to March. Look for plump, unblemished nuts that are heavy for their size. Imported canned chestnuts packed in water and pureed chestnuts are available in the gourmet section of your supermarket, as are sweetened canned chestnuts or *marron,* imported from France.

Shelled, dried chestnuts are sold in Italian, Spanish and Chinese markets. They can be used just like fresh chestnuts after soaking overnight in water to cover, then cooked until tender.

Store fresh chestnuts in a cool, dry place. They can be refrigerated for several weeks. Canned chestnuts should be refrigerated after opening. Dried chestnuts can be kept in an airtight container on the shelf.

**To Prepare:** Wash fresh chestnuts. Make a cut in the flat side of each nut to keep the nut from exploding. To shell and skin nuts, place in saucepan with water to cover; bring to boiling. Boil 3 minutes. Remove pan from heat. With spoon, remove several chestnuts and shell the nuts. Remove the inner skin from each nut. (Keep the other chestnuts in hot water until ready to shell and peel.)

**To Cook:** Fresh chestnuts can be boiled or roasted.

To serve as a vegetable, cook shelled and skinned nuts in boiling water or chicken broth in a covered saucepan over low heat until tender, about 15 minutes. Drain and serve with cooked Brussels sprouts or other green vegetable, or puree in a food processor. If using chestnuts for dessert, cook in water or sugar syrup.

To roast, place unshelled, slashed nuts in a shallow baking pan; bake in a preheated very hot oven (475°) for 15 minutes, stirring occasionally. Serve piping hot.

To roast over an open fire, use a hole-punched metal pan and roast over white coals until a nut can easily be shelled and the kernel is soft.

```
┌────────────────────────────────┐
│        Chestnut Math           │
│ 1 pound fresh chestnuts = 35 to 40 │
│  nuts = 2½ cups shelled        │
└────────────────────────────────┘
```

## CHESTNUT STUFFING

Bake at 475° for 15 minutes, then at 325° for 1 hour.
Makes about 10 cups.

- **1 pound fresh chestnuts**
  **OR: 1 can (10 ounces)**
  **water-packed chestnuts**

- **½ cup (1 stick) butter or**
  **margarine**
- **1 large onion, chopped (1 cup)**
- **1 large apple, grated (1 cup)**
- **2 cups water**
- **2 packages (8 ounces each)**
  **herb-seasoned stuffing mix**

1. Wash fresh chestnuts; cut slits in each shell; place in a shallow baking pan.
2. Bake in a preheated very hot oven (475°) for 15 minutes. Remove from pan; when cool enough to handle, shell and skin.
3. Cook shelled chestnuts, covered, in boiling salted water to cover, in a medium-size saucepan, about 5 minutes or until tender; drain; chop fine. Or, drain and chop canned chestnuts.
4. Melt butter in a large saucepan; sauté onion until soft; stir in apple and chestnuts; sauté 2 minutes. Add water; heat to boiling. Stir in stuffing mix until evenly moist.
5. Stuff turkey; or, if baking stuffing separately, spoon into a buttered 12-cup baking dish. Cover with foil.
6. Bake in a slow oven (325°) during the last hour the turkey roasts.

## CHESTNUT ICE CREAM LOG

*Honeyed chestnut-vanilla ice cream curled around green-cherry-dotted strawberry ice cream.*

Makes 10 servings.

- **1 can (15½ ounces) chestnut**
  **puree**
- **½ cup honey**
- **1 quart vanilla ice cream, softened**
- **1 quart strawberry ice cream**
- **½ cup candied green cherries,**
  **halved**

1. Line a 15½ × 10½ × 1-inch jelly-roll pan with plastic wrap.
2. Beat chestnut and honey in a large bowl with electric mixer at medium speed until smooth. Gradually beat in vanilla ice cream until no streaks of white remain. Spoon evenly into prepared pan. Freeze until firm to the touch, several hours or overnight.
3. Soften strawberry ice cream in a large bowl; spoon dollops over surface of chestnut layer; spread in an even layer; sprinkle with cherries. Roll up, beginning with short side, by

lifting up plastic wrap. (If chestnut layer cracks on rolling, wait until it softens.) Cover with plastic wrap; refreeze until very firm.
4. Transfer log to serving plate. Smooth outer surface with metal spatula. Use serrated knife or tip of fork to score surface to give rough textured look. Garnish with whipped cream, candied chestnuts, candied cherries and citron, if you wish.

———————— •●● ————————

**CHICKEN** No other food is as widely used in the world as chicken. A chicken in your shopping cart promises a good meal at a reasonable price. Dollar for dollar, chicken is hard to beat.

Chickens are descendants of a wild jungle bird from southeastern Asia, hunted by man for food as early as 1400 B.C. Some 800 years later, the Greeks and Romans were breeding the now domesticated bird not only for meat, but eggs as well. Jamestown settlers brought chickens for food and used their feathers to make beds.

Chickens have come a long way from the jungle to the barnyard to today's scientifically operated farms. Our modern birds are scientifically bred and fed a special diet to make them plump, tender and juicy. Whereas it once took months to raise a bird for market, it now takes just weeks, and the savings are reflected in the price at your supermarket. Efficient processing, Federal inspection and grading, and speedy, refrigerated transportation all guarantee carefully controlled quality of the chickens marketed today.

The chicken you buy is produced for its meat. Broiler-fryer chickens differ from egg-producing chickens the same way beef cattle differ from dairy cows.

Chicken is an excellent source of high-quality protein, rich in the essential amino acids needed for building, maintaining and replacing the body's muscles and tissues. It is low in saturated fat and lower than most meats in total fat content. A 3½-ounce serving of skinless, broiled chicken breast has only 115 calories,

185 with the skin on. It's an excellent source of niacin and iron. To learn how to carve chicken, see **CARVING**.

**Buying and Storing:** Chicken is available in a variety of types and products, fresh, frozen or canned.

*Broiler-fryer* This meaty, all-purpose chicken accounts for 90% of the chickens sold in this country. Marketed at 7 to 9 weeks old, it weighs 2 to 3½ pounds.

*Roaster* Slightly larger and older than a broiler-fryer, this chicken is marketed at 16 weeks and weighs 3½ to 6 pounds.

*Stewing chicken, hen or fowl* This chicken is mature and less tender than a broiler-fryer or roaster and is best stewed or made into soup. It may be a year or a little older. A fowl will weigh about 2½ to 3½ pounds; a stewing chicken or hen can weigh 4½ to 6 pounds.

*Capon* A male chicken that has been castrated so that it grows plump and tender. A capon weighs 4 to 7 pounds.

*Rock Cornish game hen* This is a special breed of small-size chicken that weighs 1½ pounds or less. Usually sold frozen but available fresh in some large cities, it can be roasted, broiled, fried or baked. For recipes, see **ROCK CORNISH GAME HEN**.

*Broiler-fryer chicken parts* In many markets today, it is possible to buy only those parts of the chicken you want—all breasts, for example, or thighs, drumsticks, wings or backs.

*Boneless, skinless breasts,* called chicken cutlets, are very popular.

*Chicken giblets,* which include the gizzard, liver and heart, may be used for tasty, inexpensive, nutritious dishes. For chicken liver recipes, see **PÂTÉ**.

In addition to the more familiar chicken types, new chicken products are finding their way into supermarkets—chicken frankfurters, chicken bologna, chicken luncheon meat. You will also find numerous canned, boned chicken products and frozen chicken dinners or fried parts.

**How Much to Buy:** A whole broiler-fryer is 53 percent edible. A 3-pound chicken yields approximately 3 cups cooked edible meat. In an average 3-pound bird, each breast half weighs about 7½ ounces and contains about 5 ounces of edible meat. Each wing weighs about 3½ ounces, yields 1 ounce of meat. Each drumstick weighs about 3½ ounces, yields 2 ounces of meat. Each thigh weighs about 4½ ounces, yields about 2½ ounces meat. The back-neck weighs about 8 ounces, gives only 2 ounces meat. The giblets weigh about 2 ounces each.

Here are some rules to follow in deciding how much chicken to buy. You may want to increase these portions for big eaters in the family.

*Chicken for frying:* Allow ¾ to 1 pound per serving.

*Chicken for roasting:* Allow ¾ to 1 pound per serving.

*Chicken for broiling or barbecuing:* Allow ½ chicken or 1 pound per serving.

*Chicken for stewing:* Allow ½ to 1 pound per serving.

**Storing:** Chicken, whether cut-up or whole and packed on trays, can be stored in the original wrapper. Store in the coldest part of the refrigerator and cook within 2 days. Chicken bought in bags should be removed from the bags and rinsed under cool, running water. Pat dry with paper toweling, then cut into portions desired and rewrap in foil or plastic wrap. Refrigerate and use within 2 days. If you plan to keep it for a longer period, you should freeze it.

Uncooked chicken can be frozen whole or in parts in suitable freezer wrap. Plastic freezer bags can also be used. Press all the air out of each package; seal, label and freeze for up to 6 months at 0°F.

Cooked whole chicken or parts can be wrapped as above for freezing. If the chicken was stuffed, remove stuffing and wrap separately. Chicken cooked in a sauce or gravy should be packed in a rigid container with a tight-fitting lid. Allow ½ inch at the top for expansion. Cooked chicken may be kept for up to 2 months at 0°F.

Thaw chicken in the refrigerator, or use a microwave oven. Do not refreeze thawed cooked or uncooked chicken.

**To Cook:** Chickens can be roasted, baked, broiled, sautéed, stir-fried, fried, braised, steamed, stewed or grilled.

**To Microwave:** Chicken cooks quickly on the high power setting and retains its natural juices. In general, a 3-pound whole chicken takes 1 to 1½ hours to roast in a regular oven but it will cook in less than 30 minutes in a microwave. Here are some tips for cooking chicken in a microwave oven:

● To brown chicken, coat with butter (not margarine), or use soy sauce, paprika, herbs or a commercial browning sauce.
● Do not salt chicken before cooking. Add salt during the standing time.
● Chicken parts cook best on high power, but use medium power for whole birds.
● When cooking parts, place larger, thicker parts near the outside and thinner parts toward the center of the baking dish. Place giblets under the breast.
● When in doubt about whether chicken is done, undercook rather than overcook. It's easy to return chicken for more cooking. Remember, chicken will continue to cook during the standing time.
● Because chicken cooks so quickly, added flavors are absorbed more fully if chicken is marinated before cooking.

**Cooked Chicken Safety Tips**
Since chicken is a popular picnic food, take special precautions against spoilage. See also **FOOD SAFETY**.
● Chicken that has been fried, baked or broiled with no sauce should be chilled quickly in the refrigerator before packing. It is then safe at room temperature (70°F.) for up to 4 hours.
● On warm days, pack the chicken in an insulated container or ice chest.
● Chicken salad or creamed chicken should always be kept refrigerated until eating time.

## BEER-BATTER FRIED CHICKEN

*Crispy chicken prepared with a light coating of beer batter.*

Makes 8 servings.

- **1¾ cups *sifted* all-purpose flour**
- **1½ teaspoons salt**
- **½ teaspoon pepper**
- **1 can (12 ounces) beer**
  **Vegetable oil**
- **2 broiler-fryers (2½ pounds each), cut up**

1. Combine flour, salt and pepper in a medium-size bowl. Beat in beer with a wire whisk or rotary beater until smooth. Let stand 30 minutes.
2. Pour enough vegetable oil in a large skillet or saucepan to make a 1-inch depth. Heat to 375° on a deep-fat frying thermometer or until a cube of bread turns golden within about 60 seconds.
3. Dip chicken pieces into beer batter, a few at a time, allowing excess to drain back into bowl.
4. Fry chicken pieces, turning once, for 30 minutes or until chicken tests done. Place on paper toweling to drain. Keep warm in a very slow oven (250°) until all chicken is fried. Garnish chicken with parsley and serve with onion rings, if you wish.

## DEVILED CHICKEN LEGS

*You can substitute halved chicken breasts for the chicken legs if you wish. Simply reduce broiling time by 10 minutes.*

Makes 4 servings.

- **4 chicken legs with thighs (2½ to 3 pounds)**
  **Salt and pepper**
- **¼ cup (½ stick) butter or margarine**
- **2 tablespoons hot prepared mustard**
- **½ cup white wine**
  **Dash cayenne**
- **1 teaspoon finely minced shallots or onion**
- **¾ cup packaged bread crumbs**
- **¼ cup chopped fresh parsley**

1. Cut the chicken legs about halfway through at the joint but do not sever completely. Sprinkle with salt and pepper.
2. Melt the butter in a shallow metal baking or jelly-roll pan big enough to hold legs in single layer. Add chicken and turn to coat on both sides with butter. Arrange the pieces skin-side up.
3. Broil about 4 inches from heat for 5 minutes; turn and broil another 5 minutes. Baste with butter from the pan.
4. Mix mustard, ¼ cup of the wine, cayenne and shallots or onion; spoon about half the mixture over chicken pieces. Sprinkle chicken with about one-third of the crumbs. Broil another 15 minutes.
5. Turn chicken pieces, brush with remaining mustard mixture and sprinkle with remaining crumbs. Broil another 15 minutes.
6. Lift the pieces out of pan and keep warm. Add remaining wine to baking dish and scrape sides and bottom of pan; add parsley. Spoon sauce over chicken.

## STUFFED ROAST CHICKENS

Roast at 350° for 1¾ to 2 hours.
Makes 8 servings.

- **2 tablespoons leaf rosemary, crumbled**
- **2 tablespoons leaf tarragon, crumbled**
- **⅓ cup dry white wine or chicken broth**
- **½ cup (1 stick) butter or margarine**
- **2 whole broiler-fryers (3½ pounds each)**
- **1 teaspoon salt**
- **½ teaspoon freshly ground pepper**
- **1 fresh pear, cored and chopped**
- **1 package (6 ounces) wild rice mix, cooked following label directions**

1. Combine rosemary and tarragon with wine in a small bowl; let stand 1 hour. Strain; reserve liquid. Blend butter into herbs.
2. Sprinkle cavity of each chicken with part of the salt and pepper; add 1 tablespoon herb butter. Loosen skin over breast; press in about 2 tablespoons of the herb butter.
3. Sauté chopped pear in half of remaining herb butter. Blend with cooked wild rice. Stuff chickens with wild rice; truss.
4. Melt remaining herb butter; brush over birds. Sprinkle with remaining salt and pepper. Combine the remaining herb butter with an equal amount of reserved wine or broth.
5. Roast in a moderate oven (350°) for 1¾ to 2 hours or until leg moves easily and juices are no longer pink, basting often with herb-wine mixture.
6. Serve with sautéed zucchini, broccoli, yellow squash and carrots, if you wish.

## CHICKEN PASTA PICNIC BOWL

*A colorful macaroni salad that uses the smaller pieces of chicken.*

Makes 6 to 8 servings.

- **1 package (8 ounces) elbow macaroni**
- **1 package (10 ounces) frozen peas and carrots**
- **2 cups diced cooked chicken**
- **1 cup diced Cheddar cheese**
- **½ cup sliced celery**
- **½ cup vegetable oil**
- **⅓ cup tarragon vinegar**
- **1 teaspoon salt**
- **½ teaspoon sugar**
- **½ teaspoon leaf marjoram, crumbled**
- **¼ teaspoon dry mustard**
- **¼ teaspoon pepper**
- **2 tablespoons chopped fresh parsley**
- **2 tablespoons chopped green onion**

1. Cook macaroni following label directions; drain; rinse in cold water and drain again.
2. Cook peas and carrots, following package directions, until barely tender. Drain; cool, then add to macaroni in large bowl. Add chicken, cheese and celery.
3. Combine remaining ingredients in jar with tight-fitting lid; shake vigorously until blended. Pour dressing over macaroni mixture; toss well. Chill several hours or overnight.
4. Serve with crisp lettuce and garnish with tomatoes, if you wish.

Pictured opposite: Stuffed Roast Chickens, page 171

## GREEK CHICKEN PIE

Bake at 400° for 30 minutes.
Makes 8 servings.

- **1 broiler-fryer (about 3 pounds), cut up**
- **1 teaspoon salt**
- **¼ teaspoon pepper**
- **3 cups thinly sliced carrots**
- **1½ cups sliced celery**
- **1 large onion, chopped (1 cup)**
- **1 package (9 ounces) frozen artichoke hearts**
- **½ cup (1 stick) butter**
- **6 tablespoons flour**
- **1 teaspoon salt**
- **¼ teaspoon pepper**
- **½ cup light cream**
- **2 tablespoons lemon juice**
- **½ package piecrust mix**
- **1 egg beaten with 1 tablespoon water**

1. Put chicken in large kettle or Dutch oven. Add just enough water to cover. Bring to boiling; skim off foam. Add the 1 teaspoon salt and ¼ teaspoon pepper; lower heat; cover. Simmer 30 minutes or until chicken is tender. Remove chicken from broth to a large bowl; let cool.

2. Add carrots, celery, onion and artichoke hearts to broth. Simmer until tender, 15 minutes. Drain; reserve broth and vegetables. Measure broth; add water to make 3 cups.

3. Skin and bone chicken; cut into bite-size pieces. Add vegetables to chicken.

4. Heat butter in a large saucepan; add flour and remaining salt and pepper. Cook and stir 1 minute. Stir in chicken broth and cream. Cook, stirring constantly, until thickened and bubbly. Stir in lemon juice, chicken and vegetables. Spoon into shallow 2-quart or 11 × 7 × 2-inch baking dish.

5. Preheat oven to 400°. Prepare piecrust mix following label directions. Roll out on floured surface; cut into ¾-inch strips with a pastry wheel. Fit over filling in lattice pattern. Join strips around edge of dish with an edging strip. Pinch to seal; flute. Brush pastry with egg and water.

6. Bake in a preheated hot oven (400°) for 30 minutes or until pastry is golden and filling is bubbly-hot.

*Pictured opposite: (From the top) Greek Chick-Pea Salad, page 176; Greek Chicken Pie, page 173*

# How to Cut and Bone a Chicken

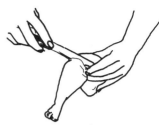

1. Place chicken breast side up. Using a sharp knife, make lengthwise slit through skin and flesh from neck to cavity. Turn bird over and repeat cut.

5. Thigh may be left attached to leg for broiling; but for frying, bend leg joint. Cut through joint with a sharp knife, separating leg from the thigh.

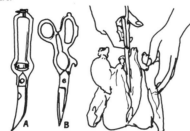

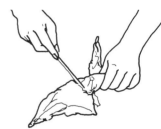

2. Using poultry shears (a) or kitchen shears (b), cut right through bones (ribs). Cutting to one side of breastbone is easier than cutting through it.

6. To separate wing from the breast, bend joint. Cut through joint with a sharp knife. The chicken will now be in eight pieces and ready for frying.

3. Turn chicken over. Cut through bones, cutting to one side of the backbone. You may remove backbone. A small bird is cut this way for serving.

7. If your recipe calls for skinned chicken breasts, use a sharp, small paring knife to start, then slip fingers between skin and flesh and peel skin.

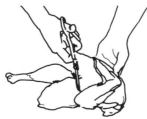

4. For quartering chicken, continue using shears. Cut across half the bird, following the natural division just below the rib cage and the breastbone.

8. To bone chicken breast, use a small paring knife. Cut meat away from rib bones with quick little strokes, feeling your way along with your fingers.

# Chicken

## EASY OVEN CHICKEN AND VEGETABLES

*Golden brown chicken with leeks and mushrooms is an easy main dish.*

Bake at 375° for 1½ hours.
Makes 6 servings.

- **2 cups sliced leeks (white part only)**
- **1 pound mushrooms**
- **2 tablespoons butter or margarine**
- **6 chicken legs (1½ pounds)**
- **6 chicken thighs (1½ pounds)**
- **¼ cup vermouth or dry white wine**
- **1 can condensed cream of mushroom soup**
- **¼ teaspoon pepper**

1. Preheat oven to 375°. Sauté leeks and mushrooms in butter in a large skillet, stirring frequently until tender, about 5 minutes. Transfer to a 13 × 9 × 2-inch baking dish.
2. Arrange chicken pieces, skin-side up, on vegetable mixture.
3. Mix wine, soup and pepper in a 2-cup measure. Pour over chicken, covering completely.
4. Bake in a preheated moderate oven (375°) for 1½ hours, basting occasionally or until chicken is tender.

## BARBECUED CHICKEN DRUMETTES

Bake at 350° for 40 minutes.
Makes 6 servings.

- **3 pounds chicken wings**
- **½ teaspoon salt**
- **¼ teaspoon pepper**
- **¼ cup vegetable oil**
- **1 large onion, chopped (1 cup)**
- **2 cloves garlic, chopped**
- **1 cup catsup**
- **½ cup apricot preserves**
- **1 tablespoon Worcestershire sauce**
- **¼ teaspoon liquid hot pepper seasoning**

1. Remove tips of chicken wings. Cut each wing into 2 pieces; sprinkle with salt and pepper. Place pieces side by side in a shallow glass dish.
2. Heat oil in a large skillet; sauté onion and garlic until golden, about 5 minutes. Stir in remaining ingredients; simmer 5 minutes. Cool and pour mixture evenly over chicken wings; chill for several hours or overnight.
3. When ready to serve, place wings in a single layer in a shallow baking pan.
4. Bake in a moderate oven (350°) for 40 minutes or until wings are tender.

## CHICKEN PROVENÇAL

Makes 4 servings.

- **2 whole chicken breasts (14 ounces each), split**
- **2 tablespoons flour**
- **½ teaspoon salt**
- **⅛ teaspoon pepper**
- **1 tablespoon butter or margarine**
- **1 tablespoon vegetable oil**
- **1 clove garlic, crushed**
- **1 small onion, chopped (¼ cup)**
- **1 can (8¼ ounces) tomatoes, drained and chopped**
- **½ cup dry white wine or chicken broth**
- **½ cup sliced pitted ripe olives**
- **2 tablespoons chopped parsley**

1. Skin and bone chicken. Flatten slightly between sheets of wax paper with rolling pin or flat side of meat mallet. Combine flour, salt and pepper on one piece of the wax paper. Turn chicken in flour to coat on all sides.
2. Heat butter and oil in large skillet. Sauté chicken 3 minutes on one side only; remove to plate.
3. Sauté garlic and onion in skillet until onion is softened, about 3 minutes. Stir in tomatoes and wine.
4. Return chicken to skillet, un-cooked-side down. Spoon some sauce over chicken. Lower heat and simmer until sauce is slightly thickened, about 5 minutes. Add olives; heat 1 more minute. Sprinkle with parsley.

## GIBLET AND BARLEY SOUP

Makes 6 servings.

- **8 ounces chicken livers (about 9), finely chopped or ground**
- **4 ounces chicken gizzards (about 6), finely chopped or ground**
- **3 envelopes or teaspoons instant chicken broth**
- **3 cups hot water**
- **¼ teaspoon pepper**
- **¼ teaspoon ground nutmeg**
- **¼ teaspoon ground cumin**
- **3 tablespoons chopped fresh parsley**
- **1 small onion, chopped (¼ cup)**
- **3 tablespoons butter or margarine**
- **½ cup barley (pearl or instant)**
- **3 cups water**
  **Salt**

1. Combine livers, gizzards, instant broth, water, pepper, nutmeg, cumin, parsley and onion in a large saucepan. Bring to boiling, cover and simmer 15 minutes.
2. Heat the butter in a large saucepan. Sauté the barley for 4 to 5 minutes, stirring and shaking the pan often. Add the water, bring to boiling, cover and simmer 30 minutes; stir occasionally.
3. Add the chicken giblet mixture, cover and cook gently about 15 minutes or until the barley is tender. Taste; add additional salt, if you wish. Serve with a hearty oatmeal bread, if you wish.

## CHICKEN DIVAN

*This classic dish is as popular as ever.*

Bake at 400° for 25 minutes.
Makes 6 servings.

- **2 packages (10 ounces each) frozen broccoli spears**
- **2 cups sliced cooked chicken**
- **¼ cup butter or margarine**
- **¼ cup all-purpose flour**
- **2 cups chicken broth**
- **½ cup heavy cream**
- **1 cup freshly grated Parmesan cheese**
- **4 teaspoons prepared mustard**
- **2 tablespoons minced onion**
- **2 tablespoons dry sherry**
- **½ teaspoon Worcestershire sauce**

1. Cook broccoli following label directions. Drain; arrange in bottom of 2-quart shallow casserole. Cut spears in half for easier serving. Arrange sliced chicken over broccoli. Preheat oven to 400°.

2. Melt butter in a medium-size saucepan; blend in flour; cook 1 minute; remove from heat. Gradually stir in chicken broth and cream. Cook, stirring constantly, until sauce thickens and bubbles 1 minute. Stir in cheese, mustard, onion, sherry and Worcestershire sauce. Continue cooking and stirring over low heat 1 minute longer. Taste; add salt and pepper, if needed. Pour sauce over chicken and broccoli.

3. Bake, uncovered, in a preheated hot oven (400°) for 25 minutes or until bubbly-hot.

## LEMON-BUTTER BROILED CHICKEN

*Chicken quarters broiled with herbs and dry wine have an outdoor grilled flavor.*

Makes 4 servings.

- **1 broiler-fryer (3 pounds), quartered**
- **1 teaspoon seasoned salt**
- **¼ teaspoon pepper**
- **¼ cup (½ stick) butter or margarine**
- **2 tablespoons lemon juice**
- **½ teaspoon leaf tarragon, crumbled**
- **½ teaspoon leaf chervil, crumbled**
- **2 tablespoons dry vermouth**

1. Sprinkle chicken quarters with salt and pepper.

2. Melt butter in small saucepan; add lemon juice, tarragon, chervil and vermouth; brush lightly over chicken quarters.

3. Place chicken, skin-side down, on rack over broiler pan.

4. Broil, 6 inches from heat, 20 minutes, basting frequently. Turn; broil 15 to 20 minutes longer or until nicely browned, brushing with remaining lemon-butter.

## CURRIED CHICKEN WITH RAISINS

*A pleasingly mild curry that's easy to prepare. Serve over rice; add fresh fruit for dessert.*

Makes 6 servings.

- **1 large onion, chopped (1 cup)**
- **½ cup chopped celery**
- **¼ cup (½ stick) butter or margarine**
- **2 teaspoons curry powder**
- **1 tablespoon flour**
- **3 tomatoes, coarsely chopped (3 cups)**
- **1 large green pepper, seeded and chopped (1 cup)**
- **¼ cup chopped fresh parsley**
- **1 teaspoon salt**
- **¼ teaspoon pepper**
- **½ cup chicken broth**
- **3 cups diced cooked chicken**
- **⅓ cup raisins**
- **¼ cup toasted slivered almonds**

1. Sauté onion and celery in butter in large skillet or Dutch oven until soft, about 5 minutes; stir in curry powder and flour; cook 1 minute. Add tomatoes and pepper; cook, stirring often, 5 minutes. Stir in parsley, salt, pepper and chicken broth; lower heat. Cover; simmer 10 minutes.

2. Add chicken and raisins; heat through. Sprinkle with almonds and serve over cooked rice, if you wish.

———— ●●● ————

**CHICORY** All parts of this native European plant were once utilized for food: young leaves eaten as salad greens, young roots cooked like parsnips. Chicory was brought to the U.S. in the late 19th century. The roots were roasted and used to supplement coffee. The use of chicory with coffee declined as coffee became more readily available. The French and their descendants, particularly in New Orleans, are still fond of the blend.

Chicory used for greens, also known as curly endive, is cultivated or can be gathered from the wild. Chicory greens are bitter tasting, the leaves are dark green and somewhat serrated.

Another variety of chicory is called *witloof,* a Dutch word meaning white leaf. Witloof is commonly called Belgian endive. It is used in salads or can be cooked as a vegetable. For more information, see **ENDIVE.**

**CHICK-PEAS** Widely used in the Mediterranean, chick-peas are nutritious ivory-hued beans. Spaniards and Mexicans call them *garbanzo beans,* Italians call them *ceci,* and the Arabs call them *hommos* or *hummus.*

Chick-peas are the seeds of a bushy plant that grows in dry regions. Although three varieties are grown, only one is widely used.

Chick-peas are available dried in one-pound packages or sold in bulk by the pound. They are also cooked and canned in 16- or 20-ounce-size cans. To cook dried chick-peas, see **BEANS.**

Use chick-peas in soups, stews, salads and mashed as an appetizer dip.

## STUFFED PEPPERS, ITALIAN-STYLE

*Chick-peas are the stretcher here instead of the usual rice.*

Bake at 350° for 20 minutes.
Makes 6 servings.

- **6 medium-size green peppers**
- **1 pound ground round or chuck**
- **1 large onion, chopped (1 cup)**
- **1 teaspoon salt**
- **½ teaspoon fennel seeds, crushed**
- **1 can (16 ounces) chick-peas, (garbanzo beans), drained**
- **1 egg**
- **1 teaspoon leaf oregano, crumbled**
- **¼ cup minced fresh parsley**
- **1 package (8 ounces) mozzarella cheese, diced**
- **1 can (15 ounces) tomato sauce**

1. Cut a slice from top of each pepper; scoop out seeds and membranes. Parboil peppers in a small amount of boiling water 10 minutes; drain well. Stand in a greased shallow baking pan that just fits them. Preheat oven to 350°.

2. Brown beef with onion, salt and fennel in a large skillet, stirring often to break up beef. Spoon off all fat. Remove from heat.

3. Add chick-peas, egg, oregano, parsley and cheese; toss gently to mix. Spoon into pepper cups. Drizzle tomato sauce over and around stuffed peppers. Cover pan with foil.

4. Bake in a preheated moderate oven (350°) for 20 minutes or until bubbly and hot.

# Chick-Peas

## GREEK CHICK-PEA SALAD

*Here is a delicious salad which only takes a few minutes to prepare. It can be assembled early in the day, and the cheese and garnish added just before serving.*

Makes 8 to 10 servings.

2 teaspoons Dijon
  mustard
1½ teaspoons salt
1¼ cups olive or vegetable oil
½ cup lemon juice
¼ teaspoon ground pepper
2 cans (20 ounces each)
  chick-peas, drained
1 medium-size red onion, sliced
  and separated into rings
4 ounces feta cheese,
  crumbled
2 tablespoons chopped fresh
  parsley
  Lettuce leaves

1. Combine mustard, salt, oil, lemon juice and pepper in container of electric blender; whirl until smooth. (Or, shake well in a 1-quart screw-top jar.)
2. Combine chick-peas and onion in a large bowl. Pour dressing over and toss. Refrigerate 1 hour. (May be prepared several days in advance.)
3. Just before serving, add cheese and parsley; toss. Spoon into lettuce-lined salad bowl.

## CHICK-PEA DIP

Makes 2 cups.

¼ cup sesame seeds
2 tablespoons water
½ teaspoon vegetable oil
3 tablespoons lemon
  juice
1 clove garlic, crushed
¼ teaspoon ground cumin
1 can (16 ounces) chick-peas,
  undrained
  Chopped fresh parsley
  Assorted raw vegetables

1. Place sesame seeds in container of electric blender or food processor; whirl until ground. Add water and oil; whirl until smooth paste forms.
2. Add lemon juice, garlic and cumin. Drain chick-peas, reserving liquid. Add chick-peas to sesame mixture; whirl until smooth. Add as much liquid as is necessary to make a dip consistency.
3. Pour dip into a small serving bowl; cover and chill several hours.
4. To serve: Place bowl of dip on a large plate. Garnish dip with chopped parsley. Surround bowl with raw vegetables—celery or carrot sticks, cherry tomatoes, edible-podded peas, green or red pepper strips, broccoli or cauliflowerets.

## BASQUE GARBANZO CASSEROLE

*A simplified version of the* Olla Podrida, *the popular Spanish soup-stew.*

Bake at 325° for 1 hour.
Makes 8 servings.

½ pound piece pepperoni,
  sliced
1 whole chicken breast (about 12
  ounces)
1 large leek, chopped
2 cloves garlic, minced
4 medium-size carrots,
  sliced
2 cups shredded cabbage
  (¼ head)
2 cans (20 ounces each)
  chick-peas (garbanzo beans),
  drained
1 can (16 ounces) tomatoes
3 teaspoons salt
1 teaspoon leaf thyme,
  crumbled
½ teaspoon pepper

1. Sauté pepperoni in a large skillet for 5 minutes; remove with slotted spoon. Cut chicken breast into 2-inch pieces through bone with poultry shears. Or, bone chicken and cut into pieces.
2. Brown chicken pieces in pan drippings; remove with slotted spoon. Sauté leek and garlic in pan drippings; stir in carrots and cook 3 minutes; stir in cabbage and cook 2 minutes. Add chick-peas, tomatoes, salt, thyme and pepper; stir to blend well. Preheat oven to 325°.
3. Spoon the chick-pea mixture, browned chicken and pepperoni into a 12-cup baking dish. Cover.
4. Bake in a preheated slow oven (325°) for 1 hour.

— ••• —

## CHILDREN CAN COOK

Calling all kids! Cooking can be lots of fun, and your parents will be pleased with the good foods you can learn to prepare. With our step-by-step drawings, you will be able to make a delicious dinner all by yourself. But before you begin, read this important information.

### Play It Safe In the Kitchen

● Learn how to correctly use the oven and the surface of your range. Have a parent show you how to turn on the heat and how to control the heat.
● Use a *dry* potholder to hold pan handles and racks and to remove foods from the oven. A wet potholder will get hot during use.
● Always turn pan handles toward the back of the range so the pan cannot be tipped or pulled over.
● Use a wooden spoon to stir hot foods.

### Basic Recipe for All Cooks

● Read the recipe first. Before you begin, be sure you have all the needed ingredients and equipment on hand.
● Wash hands in soap and hot water.
● Measure all the ingredients carefully. That way the recipes turn out right every time.
● Do everything just as the recipe says to do it. Don't substitute or change ingredients.
● Clean up the kitchen and all utensils when you are finished—then your parents will be happy to let you cook another day!

### Menu for Four

Tacos Olé*
Chewy Chocolate Squares*
Strawberry Ice Cream
Milk
*Recipe follows

### Timetable For Menu

1. Day before, do all grocery shopping.
2. About 2 hours before dinner, prepare Chewy Chocolate Squares (page 178) so that they can cool.
3. About 1 hour before dinner, make Tacos Olé (next page).

## Shopping List

- 1 small head lettuce
- 1 large tomato
- 1 package (4 ounces) shredded Cheddar cheese
- 1 can (8 ounces) tomato sauce
- 1 pound ground chuck
- 1 envelope (1¼ ounces) taco seasoning mix
- 1 package (5 ounces) taco shells (10 shells)
- 1 package graham cracker crumbs
- 1 can (14 ounces) sweetened condensed milk *(not evaporated milk)*
- 1 package (6 ounces) semisweet chocolate pieces
- 1 package walnut pieces
- 1 pint strawberry ice cream

### Have On Hand

salt
instant minced onion
vegetable shortening
milk for drinking

## TACOS OLÉ

### Ingredients

- ½ head lettuce
- 1 large tomato
- 1 package (4 ounces) shredded Cheddar cheese (1 cup)
- 1 can (8 ounces) tomato sauce
- 1 pound ground chuck
- 2 tablespoons instant minced onion
- 1 envelope (1¼ ounces) taco seasoning mix
- 1 cup water
- 1 package (5 ounces) taco shells (10 shells)

### Utensils Needed

sharp knife
cutting board
1 medium bowl
3 small bowls
can opener
large skillet
long-handled wooden spoon
cookie sheet
tongs
4 dinner plates
large serving dish

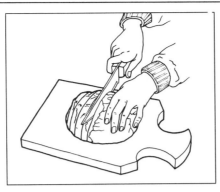

1. Wash lettuce with cold water; drain on paper toweling. Cut the lettuce into ½-inch strips on cutting board. Put lettuce into medium bowl.

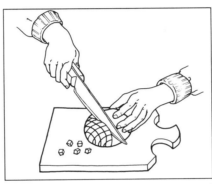

2. Wash tomato. Cut out stem end and cut tomato in half. Cut tomato into ½-inch pieces. Put into small bowl. Put the cheese into other small bowl. Open tomato sauce with can opener and pour into small bowl.

3. Crumble the ground chuck into skillet. Cook over medium heat while stirring with spoon until meat is brown. Add the onion, taco seasoning mix and water. Turn heat to low. Cook 15 minutes or until meat is almost dry.

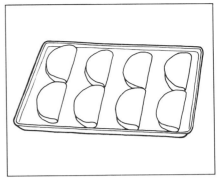

4. While meat cooks, turn oven to 250°. Place taco shells on cookie sheet. Bake 5 minutes or just until warm.

5. Use tongs to remove shells to dinner plates. Put meat mixture into serving dish.

6. To serve: Spoon a couple of tablespoons of meat mixture into shells. Add cheese, lettuce and tomato. Serve with tomato sauce.

# Children Can Cook

## CHEWY CHOCOLATE SQUARES

### Ingredients

1½ cups graham cracker
    crumbs
1 can (14 ounces) sweetened
    condensed milk
1 package (6 ounces) semisweet
    chocolate pieces
½ cup walnut pieces
½ teaspoon salt
1 pint strawberry ice cream
    (optional)

### Utensils Needed

square baking pan (9 × 9 × 2-inch)
wax paper
large bowl
wooden spoon
wire rack
small knife

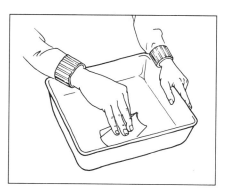

1. Turn oven to 350°. Grease baking pan with some vegetable shortening using a small piece of wax paper.

2. Combine graham cracker crumbs, milk, chocolate, walnuts and salt in a large bowl with wooden spoon.

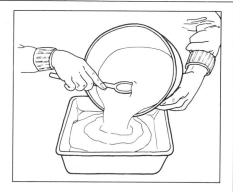

3. Pour mixture into pan; spread to an even layer.
4. Bake for 25 minutes. Cool in pan on wire rack. Cut into 16 squares. (Serve leftover squares for snacks.)
5. Serve squares with ice cream if you like.

## PIZZA POPCORN

Makes 12 cups.

½ cup (1 stick) butter or
    margarine
½ teaspoon leaf oregano,
    crumbled
½ teaspoon garlic salt
½ teaspoon leaf basil, crumbled
⅛ teaspoon crushed red pepper
12 cups freshly popped popcorn
2 tablespoons grated Parmesan
    cheese

1. Melt butter in a small saucepan; stir in oregano, garlic salt, basil and crushed pepper. Heat 1 minute.
2. Pour over popcorn in a large bowl; sprinkle with Parmesan; toss lightly until coated.

## PEANUT BUTTER MUNCHIES

*No cooking and only one mixing bowl.*

Makes about 3 dozen.

1¼ cups graham cracker crumbs
1 cup *unsifted* 10X
    (confectioners') sugar
1 cup cream-style peanut butter
¼ cup (½ stick) butter or
    margarine, softened
½ cup chopped walnuts
½ cup flaked coconut

1. Mix graham cracker crumbs, 10X sugar, peanut butter and butter in a medium-size bowl, using wooden spoon.

2. Roll between palms to shape into small balls. Roll half of the balls in nuts and other half in coconut. Refrigerate.

## COOKIE A-B-C's

Bake at 350° for 10 minutes.
Makes about 20 letters.

1 package (17 ounces)
    refrigerated slice-and-bake
    sugar cookie dough
    Milk
    Colored sugar or nonpareiles

1. Lightly grease cookie sheet. Slice cookie dough into ½-inch widths. Roll to 12-inch length with palms on wax paper. Preheat oven to 350°.
2. Place on prepared cookie sheet; shape into letters about 4-inches high. (Some letters take more than 1 strip.)
3. Brush dough lightly with milk so sugar will stick. Sprinkle with colored sugar or nonpareiles.
4. Bake in a preheated moderate oven (350°) for 10 minutes. Let cool 1 minute. Remove to wire rack using wide spatula.

## GRANOLA

Bake at 300° for 20 minutes.
Makes 6 cups.

3 cups rolled oats
⅓ cup firmly packed brown sugar
½ teaspoon salt
½ cup vegetable oil
1 cup dried apples, cut in half
1 cup raisins
½ cup walnuts
⅓ cup shelled sunflower seeds
⅓ cup shelled pumpkin seeds
2 tablespoons sesame seeds

1. Combine rolled oats, brown sugar, salt and oil in a large bowl.
2. Add apples, raisins, walnuts, sunflower seeds, pumpkin seeds and sesame seeds to oat mixture, stirring thoroughly. Spread mixture in a jelly-roll pan or rimmed cookie sheet.
3. Bake in a slow oven (300°) for 20 minutes, turning once. Remove pan to wire rack. Let cool thoroughly. Store granola in tightly covered container.

●●●

**CHILE** (also **chili, chilli** or **chilie**) To say chile is synonymous with Mexican cooking is not entirely correct. A lot of chiles are used in dishes from Mexico, but chiles are also used in Africa, India, Southeast Asia, China, Japan, some Pacific Islands, Spain and Italy. It is used fresh or dried and ground.

Chile is a species of *Capsicum* (the pepper family) which includes the green pepper (sometimes called bell or sweet pepper). A variety of small red chile when dried and ground is called ground red pepper or cayenne. Though it is used like black pepper, it is not related to peppercorns at all. See **PEPPERCORNS**.

Identifying chiles is a problem because there are so many varieties; moreover, one variety which is mild when grown in certain soil may become a hot chile when grown elsewhere. Basically, we can divide chiles into two categories: mild and hot. Mild green chiles include the 6-inch-long *Anaheim* or *California* chile, and the longer *Mild New Mexico* chile. Hot chiles include Jalapeño, Serrano, Poblano, Mulato, Guero and Fresno. *Jalapeño* is dark green and about 2½ inches long. *Serrano* is also dark green but only 1½-inches long. *Poblano* is shaped like a small, triangular green pepper but is black-green in color. *Mulato* is shaped like Poblano, but is larger and darker in color. *Guero* is yellow, about 3-inches long. *Fresno* is bright green and looks like Jalapeño but is wider and bigger.

Other vegetables on the market may look like chiles but may be sweet frying peppers. In some markets you'll find a slender 5-inch-long green or reddish-orange pepper called a hot pepper and not a chile. For more information, see **PEPPER**.

Chiles may be dried when ripe. They are sold whole or can be ground. *Ancho* or dried *pasilla* is the most popular, sold whole or ground. *Ground chile* should not be confused with *chili powder,* which is a blend of spices. *Chipotle* is a 2-inch chile that's very hot in flavor. Chile *tepin,* which are ¼-inch-round chiles, and chile *pe-*

*quin,* which are tiny oval-shaped chiles, are extremely hot. *Hapaka* is a very hot dried Japanese chile. Also on the market are crushed red peppers, used in Italian or Chinese recipes, and whole small red peppers, used primarily for pickling.

**Buying and Storing**: When buying fresh chiles, select firm, plump unblemished ones. Store in plastic bags and refrigerate. Store all dried chiles in a very cool dry place or refrigerate.

Mild green chiles and Jalapeños are usually canned in a mild brine or pickled. Refrigerate canned chiles when opened.

**To Prepare**: When handling fresh or canned chiles, you may want to wear rubber gloves. Capsaicin, the substance which gives the chile its hotness, is found concentrated in the tissue to which the seeds are attached. When cleaning chiles, handle that part carefully. Chiles should be seeded and deveined before use. Usually only the long, mild chiles are peeled before use. To peel, heat chiles over a gas flame or under a broiler until the skin blisters and browns. Drop into a plastic bag; when cool, peel, seed, devein and rinse in water. Pat dry with paper toweling before using.

**CHILI** Nowadays real chili is difficult to find. In fact, if you want it, you'll probably have to make it yourself! Each region of the U.S. has its own version—and you'll encounter a wide range of recipes clear across the country.

Many people think of chili as a spicy ground meat sauce or a pinto bean stew with meat and chili powder. Good chili is neither. A steaming hot bowl of chili should be made of diced or coarsely chopped beef—not ground beef—simmered with onion, garlic, oregano, cumin and ground dried red chile, not chili powder.

Most of the chili powder sold in this country is a mixture of such spices as cumin, garlic powder, oregano and ground chile.

The actual translation of *chili con carne* is "chili with meat," so there

should not be any beans in the recipe. Yet so often you find chili laced with boiled pinto or even kidney beans. Authentic chili does not have beans in it, although beans may be served alongside.

**RANCH-STYLE CHILI**

*A really fine chili, cooked the way Texans like it. Serve with beans, if you like, but never add them to the chili.*

Makes 8 servings.

- **4 tablespoons vegetable oil**
- **3 pounds beef chuck or round, cut into ¼- to ½-inch cubes**
- **2 large onions, chopped (2 cups)**
- **3 cloves garlic, finely minced**
- **2 tablespoons ground red chile**
  OR: **4 tablespoons chili powder**
- **2 tablespoons flour**
- **3 teaspoons cumin seeds, crushed**
- **2 teaspoons leaf oregano, crumbled**
- **2 teaspoons salt**
- **⅛ to ¼ teaspoon cayenne**
- **1 can condensed beef broth**
- **1½ cups water**
- **1 to 2 tablespoons cornmeal**

1. Heat 2 tablespoons of the oil in a heavy Dutch oven; add meat to brown lightly, ⅓ at a time; remove as it browns. Add onions and garlic to pan, adding more oil as needed; sauté until tender and lightly browned, 10 minutes. Return all meat to pan.
2. Combine ground chile, flour and cumin; sprinkle mixture over meat; stir with wooden spoon over low heat until meat is evenly coated, 1 to 2 minutes. Stir in oregano, salt, cayenne, beef broth and water. Bring to boiling, stirring often. Lower heat; simmer slowly, covered, 1½ to 2 hours or until meat is very tender.
3. Sprinkle in the cornmeal, stirring constantly; cook until slightly thickened, 5 to 10 minutes. Serve with freshly cooked hot rice and cooked pinto beans, if you wish.

———————————— •●● ————————————

**CHINESE CABBAGE** See **CABBAGE**.

# Chinese Cooking

**CHINESE COOKING** In the same way that America has many distinct styles of cooking, so does China—all delicious and well worth trying. Stir-frying is just one of the many cooking methods. There's also steaming, red-cooking or braising, deep frying, stewing, boiling and roasting.

The Cantonese style of cooking is most familiar to people in this country, probably because the Cantonese were the first immigrants. Canton, a city in southern China, has an abundance of fresh produce, seafood, rice, poultry and pork.

Cooking in northern China is based on wheat dishes—noodles, steamed buns and flat pancakes—rather than on rice. Light, delicate dishes are preferred.

In western China—the Szechuan and Hunan provinces—the food is hot and spicy. It is laced with hot peppers, ginger, garlic and peppercorns.

Shanghai, to the east, has still another style of cooking. Red-cooking—braising meats in soy sauce and sugar—is a specialty. Seafood, green tea and vinegar are abundant in this area.

For more information, see **BEAN SPROUTS, CABBAGE, SOY SAUCE, STIR-FRY, TOFU, WOK.**

## STIR-FRIED SHRIMP

*A hot and spicy Szechuan dish typical of cooking in western China.*

Makes 4 servings.

- 1 **pound medium-size shrimp, shelled and deveined**
  OR: ½ **pound frozen shelled and deveined shrimp, thawed**
- 1 **egg white**
- 2 **teaspoons cornstarch**
- ½ **teaspoon salt**
- 2 **cups peanut or corn oil**
  **Sherry Sauce**
  **(recipe follows)**
- 2 **teaspoons minced fresh ginger**
  OR: ½ **teaspoon ground ginger**
- 1 **clove garlic, minced**
  **(½ teaspoon)**
- ¼ **to ½ teaspoon crushed red pepper**

1. Split shrimp in half lengthwise; rinse; dry on paper toweling. Combine egg white, cornstarch and salt in medium-size bowl. Add shrimp and toss until coated. Refrigerate 1 to 24 hours.
2. Heat oil in wok or deep skillet until temperature is 300° on deep-fat frying thermometer. Add shrimp; stir-fry 1 to 2 minutes or until shrimp changes color and pieces separate. Pour shrimp and oil into strainer placed over a bowl. (May be prepared an hour ahead of time to this point.)
3. Prepare Sherry Sauce.
4. Reheat wok; return 2 tablespoons of the drained oil to the wok. Add ginger; stir-fry 5 seconds. Add garlic and pepper; stir-fry 5 seconds. Add shrimp; stir-fry until heated throughout, about 1 minute.
5. Stir Sherry Sauce to combine; pour into wok, stirring until sauce thickens and coats shrimp with a clear glaze. Serve with hot cooked rice, if you wish.

**Sherry Sauce:** Combine 1 teaspoon sugar, 1 teaspoon cornstarch, 2 tablespoons soy sauce, 1 tablespoon dry sherry, 1 tablespoon water and 1 teaspoon vinegar in a cup. Stir well.

## CHINESE ALMOND COOKIES

*These crisp cookies, served with sherbet, make a delightful ending to a heavy meal. They also make a delicious between-meal snack.*

Bake at 325° for 15 minutes.
Makes 4 dozen cookies.

- ⅓ **cup butter, softened**
- ⅓ **cup vegetable shortening**
- ½ **cup sugar**
- 1½ **cups** *sifted* **all-purpose flour**
- 1½ **teaspoons baking powder**
- ¼ **teaspoon salt**
- 1 **tablespoon milk**
- ½ **teaspoon almond extract**
- 2 **egg whites**
  **Granulated sugar**
  **Whole blanched almonds**

1. Combine butter, shortening and sugar in a large bowl. Beat until fluffy-light. Preheat oven to 325°.
2. Sift flour, baking powder and salt onto wax paper. Add flour mixture to butter mixture alternately with milk and almond extract.
3. Beat egg whites in a small bowl until soft peaks form; fold into mixture.
4. Measure teaspoon-size pieces of dough and shape into balls. Roll in granulated sugar and place on a greased cookie sheet. Press a whole almond into the center of each.
5. Bake in a preheated slow oven (325°) 15 minutes. Cool on wire rack.

## VELVET SLICED CHICKEN

Makes 4 servings.

- 1 **chicken breast (about 14 ounces), halved**
- 8 **egg whites (1 cup)**
- 3 **tablespoons cornstarch**
- 1 **teaspoon salt**
- ¾ **cup chicken broth**
- 2 **cups peanut or corn oil**
- ¼ **pound fresh snow peas, halved**
  OR: ½ **a 7-ounce package frozen snow peas**
- 1 **tablespoon dry sherry**
- ½ **teaspoon sugar**
- 2 **tablespoons minced cooked bacon or ham**
  **Green onion**

1. Skin and bone chicken. Flatten pieces between sheets of wax paper to ⅛-inch thickness using a meat mallet or rolling pin. Cut breast pieces in half lengthwise, then cut into 1-inch pieces to make 1 × 1 × ⅛-inch slices (about ¾ cup).
2. Beat egg whites in large bowl with rotary beater until foamy. Stir in chicken.
3. Combine cornstarch and salt in a small bowl; stir in chicken broth slowly until blended. Pour into chicken mixture.
4. Heat oil in wok or skillet to 300° on deep-fat frying thermometer. Stir chicken mixture; pour into hot oil.
5. Turn mixture gently with slotted spoon as egg white sets and chicken turns white (about 2 minutes).
6. Pour oil and chicken into strainer placed over a bowl to drain.
7. Wipe wok clean. Return 1 tablespoon of the oil to wok; reheat. Place chicken mixture and snow peas in wok; stir-fry 1 minute. Sprinkle with sherry and sugar. Stir 1 more minute. Sprinkle with bacon; garnish with green onion.

Pictured opposite: (Clockwise from the top) Glazed Beef, page 182; Stir-Fried Shrimp, page 180; Velvet Sliced Chicken, page 180; Pork Omelets, page 183.

# Chinese Cooking

## WALNUT CHICKEN

*This fast-cooking Cantonese recipe is nutty and flavorful.*

Makes 4 servings.

- 1 tablespoon cornstarch
- 3 tablespoons soy sauce
- 1 tablespoon dry sherry
- ½ teaspoon ground ginger
- 1 pound boneless chicken breasts, cut into 1-inch pieces
- 4 tablespoons vegetable oil
- ⅓ cup sliced green onions (1-inch long)
- 1 clove garlic, minced
- ½ pound fresh snow peas, tips and strings removed
  OR: 1 package (7 ounces) frozen snow peas, partially thawed
- 1 cup walnut pieces

1. Combine cornstarch, soy sauce, sherry and ginger in a medium-size bowl; add chicken pieces; let stand 15 minutes.
2. Meanwhile, heat wok or large skillet; add 3 tablespoons of the oil; heat until smoking; add green onions, garlic and snow peas. Cook 3 minutes, stirring mixture with slotted spoon. Remove mixture to a bowl.
3. Add remaining oil to wok; heat; add chicken pieces and soy mixture. Stir-fry chicken pieces until done and soy mixture begins to coat chicken, about 5 minutes. Add walnuts and vegetable mixture. Toss until mixed. Serve with hot cooked rice, if you wish.

## SHRIMP TOAST

*In America, Shrimp Toast is very popular as an appetizer. In China, it is used as one of the many dishes in a banquet, usually served after four to eight cold dishes. It is prepared in all provinces.*

Makes 24 pieces.

- 1 package (8 ounces) frozen, shelled and deveined shrimp, thawed
- 4 canned water chestnuts, finely minced
- 1 egg, slightly beaten
- 1 teaspoon salt
- ½ teaspoon sugar
- 1 teaspoon dry sherry
- 1 tablespoon cornstarch
- 6 slices of bread, at least two days old
- 2 cups vegetable oil

1. Chop shrimp until paste-like. Mix with water chestnuts, egg, salt, sugar, sherry and cornstarch.
2. Trim crusts from bread and cut each slice into 4 triangles. Spread a teaspoon of the shrimp mixture over each triangle.
3. In a saucepan, heat oil to 375°. Gently lower 4 to 6 pieces at a time into the oil, shrimp side down. (Filling will not fall off.) After about a minute, when the edges begin to turn brown, turn pieces over and fry a few more seconds. Remove; drain on paper toweling. Keep warm in very low oven until ready to serve.
*Note:* Shrimp Toast can also be fried, then frozen. When ready to use, heat in a 400° oven for 10 to 12 minutes.

## CHINESE ROAST PORK

Bake at 350° for 35 minutes then at 450° for 15 minutes.

Makes 12 servings as an appetizer or 6 servings as a main dish.

- 3 pounds lean pork butt or pork shoulder
- ⅓ cup dry sherry
- 2 cloves garlic, crushed
- 3 tablespoons dark soy sauce
- ½ cup catsup
- 3 tablespoons dark brown sugar
- 1 teaspoon salt
- 8 drops red food coloring
- ¼ cup honey

1. Cut pork into strips about 5 × 1 × 1 inches.
2. Combine remaining ingredients, except honey, in a large flat pan. Marinate pork in sauce for at least 4 hours in the refrigerator, turning occasionally.
3. After marinating, preheat oven to 350°. Drain pork and brush each piece with honey. Arrange on wire rack over foil-lined roasting pan.
4. Bake in a preheated moderate oven (350°) for 35 minutes. Turn heat to very hot (450°); bake 15 to 20 minutes longer, brushing occasionally with reserved marinade. Cool pork and slice.

## GLAZED BEEF

Makes 4 servings.

- ¾ pound boneless round steak, cut ¾-inch thick
- 1 egg white
- 2 tablespoons cornstarch
- 2 tablespoons soy sauce
- 4 cups water
- ¾ pound small zucchini (1½-inch diameter)
- 1 teaspoon cornstarch
- ½ teaspoon sugar
- 1 tablespoon cold water
- 1½ tablespoons soy sauce
- 3 tablespoons peanut or corn oil

1. Cut the beef into ¼-inch slices, then into 1-inch pieces. (This makes about 1½ cups of 1 × ¾ × ¼-inch pieces.)
2. Combine egg white and the 2 tablespoons cornstarch in medium-size bowl with fork. Add beef and the 2 tablespoons soy sauce; mix well, using your hands. Refrigerate 30 minutes.
3. Bring water to boiling in large saucepan. Add the beef and egg white mixture, stirring gently to separate the pieces, about 1 minute. Drain immediately; cool in a bowl of cold water. Drain; place on paper toweling. (May be done several hours ahead of time.)
4. Cut zucchini into 1-inch slices, then turn onto flat side; cut into ¼-inch slices to make about 3 cups of 1½ × 1 × ¼-inch pieces. Reserve.
5. Make sauce by combining remaining 1 teaspoon cornstarch, ½ teaspoon sugar, 1 tablespoon cold water and remaining 1½ tablespoons soy sauce in small cup.
6. Heat a wok or skillet until very hot. Add oil. Place zucchini in oil; stir-fry 1 minute. Increase heat and add drained beef. Mix quickly. Stir in reserved sauce, stirring until the sauce thickens and coats the beef with a clear glaze. Serve with hot cooked rice, if you wish.
*Note:* Parboiled broccoli or cauliflowerets sliced 2 inches long may be used instead of the zucchini. One teaspoon chopped fresh ginger may be added to oil before the vegetables and meat.

# Chocolate

## CHICKEN AND CHINESE CABBAGE SALAD

Makes 4 servings.

- **1 chicken breast (about 12 ounces)**
- **1 package (7 ounces) frozen snow peas**
- **¼ cup peanut or vegetable oil**
- **2 tablespoons cider vinegar**
- **4½ teaspoons soy sauce**
- **¾ teaspoon ground ginger**
  **Pinch sugar and salt**
- **¼ cup sliced green onions**
- **1 cup fresh mung bean sprouts**
- **1 small head Chinese celery cabbage**
- **1 tablespoon toasted sesame seeds**
- **½ cup coarsely chopped walnuts**

1. Simmer chicken breast in salted water until tender, about 10 minutes. Skin, bone and cube (1½ cups).
2. Defrost snow peas; dry on paper toweling.
3. To make a dressing, shake oil, vinegar, soy sauce, ginger, sugar and salt in a screw-top jar.
4. Toss chicken, snow peas, green onions and bean sprouts with the soy dressing; cover and refrigerate.
5. Slice enough cabbage to make 4 cups. Place in bowl; arrange chicken mixture on top. Sprinkle sesame seeds and walnuts over top. Toss.

## PORK OMELETS

*The shape and color of these tiny omelets resemble gold nuggets and are a symbol of wealth for the New Year. This is a simplified version of the traditional dish from the Eastern region of China.*

Makes 4 servings.

- **1 pound Chinese celery cabbage OR: 1 package (10 ounces) frozen green peas**
- **4 eggs**
- **¼ pound ground pork or beef**
- **1 teaspoon cornstarch**
- **1 tablespoon soy sauce**
- **1 tablespoon dry sherry**
- **1 green onion, finely chopped**
- **3 to 4 tablespoons vegetable oil**
- **1 cup chicken broth (see Note below)**
- **1 teaspoon salt**

- **½ teaspoon sugar**

1. Cut cabbage into 2 × 1-inch strips (about 4 cups).
2. Beat eggs in large bowl with rotary beater until frothy. Add pork, cornstarch, soy sauce, sherry and onion. Stir with fork to make sure pork is in very small pieces.
3. Heat large skillet; add 1 tablespoon of the oil. Pour egg mixture by tablespoonfuls into skillet to make 2½-inch omelets. Make 4 or 5 at a time. Cook about 2 minutes or just until most of the egg is set. While omelets are still soft, fold in half, using a small spatula. Press lightly, then turn and cook 1 more minute. Remove to platter. Continue with remaining mixture and use as much oil as is necessary. (Makes about 24 omelets.)
4. Wipe skillet clean; reheat and add 2 tablespoons of the oil. Stir-fry cabbage 2 minutes. Add chicken broth, salt and sugar. Stir well.
5. Arrange omelets on top of cabbage. Cover; cook until cabbage is just tender, about 5 minutes. Serve with hot cooked rice, if you wish.
*Note:* If peas are used, decrease the amount of chicken broth to ½ cup.

———— •●● ————

**CHIVES** Chives grow from tiny bulbs in grass-like clumps. They are noted for their delicate onion flavor and fresh, spring-green color. Most supermarkets now sell them in the spring or summer in little flowerpots. When they are 6 to 8 inches high, snip them off with scissors and add to salads, soups, scrambled eggs, salad dressing, mashed or baked potatoes and cottage cheese. The plant will continue to grow, providing you with another crop to harvest.

If chives are allowed to flower, the result will be clover-like rose-colored buds. The flowers can be cut and tossed into a green salad.

Another different variety of chives found in some markets is called "garlic" or "Chinese chives." They look much like other chives, but their leaves are flatter and wider. Garlic chives have a mild garlic flavor. Their flowers are white.

Fresh chives can be preserved by drying or freezing. To dry in a microwave oven, place washed and cut chives on a piece of doubled paper toweling. Microwave 1½ minutes on high power or until dry. Store in jar at room temperature. To freeze, wash, cut and put chives in small, airtight containers. Label, date and freeze. Commercially frozen chopped chives and freeze-dried chives are readily available.

**CHOCOLATE** There's no question that one of America's most beloved flavors is chocolate. Chocolate has a unique, satisfying and sensuous taste, and is enjoyed in many forms.

Chocolate is a product of the New World. As early as the 16th century, Mexicans were already enjoying a frothy chocolate drink and the Spanish invaders under Cortez took the dark brown mystery product back to Europe. Hot chocolate in particular became an instant favorite. It wasn't long before there were chocolate shops galore where people went to enjoy a cup of the brew.

Chocolate is produced from cacao beans. Cacao beans are the seeds of a large, oval fruit. The fruit grows directly on the main branches of the cacao tree. Each fruit contains about 25 to 40 olive-size seeds or beans. The seeds are removed from the pulp and dried. Then they are roasted and ground until the fat in them liquifies. The rich dark liquid is unsweetened chocolate. Cacao beans are also called cocoa beans.

In Colonial America, chocolate was imported from Europe until the first chocolate factory in Massachusetts started production in 1765. No other people in the world have explored cooking with chocolate to the extent that Americans have. We pride ourselves on our luscious, mind-boggling recipes for chocolate cakes, pies, desserts, cookies and candies. For more recipes, see **CANDY, COOKIE, DESSERT, PIE.**

### Chocolate Products

*Unsweetened chocolate* is the basic chocolate from which all other

# Chocolate

products are made. Roasted cocoa beans are pressed in special machines until the cocoa butter liquefies; the resulting chocolate liquor is then poured into molds to harden into cakes of pure chocolate, each weighing 1 ounce.

*Cocoa* is made by processing the chocolate liquor to remove most of the cocoa butter. The resulting mass is cooled, pulverized and sifted to produce unsweetened cocoa. *Breakfast cocoa* has slightly more cocoa butter than plain cocoa. "*Dutch*" *cocoa* has been treated with an alkali that darkens the cocoa and gives it a characteristic taste.

*Semisweet chocolate* is a blend of unsweetened chocolate, sugar and cocoa butter.

*Semisweet chocolate pieces,* also called bits or chips, are a blend of unsweetened chocolate, sugar and cocoa butter, specially formulated to hold their shape softly when baked. Milk chocolate pieces are also available.

*Sweet cooking chocolate* is a lighter and milder blend of unsweetened chocolate, sugar and cocoa butter. It's sold as 4-ounce bars.

*Liquid chocolate* is an unsweetened liquid product with a cocoa base that is available in 1-ounce packets.

*Chocolate syrup* is a ready-to-use sweetened product with a cocoa base. *Cocoa beverage mixes* are generally a blend of cocoa, sugar and dry milk. They are convenient for making hot or cold beverages.

*Milk chocolate* is sweet chocolate with milk added and comes in the familiar candy bar.

*Chocolate substitutes* such as chocolate-flavored chips are fairly new products that do not contain chocolate, but do have a cocoa base and vegetable fats added. Check labels for uses.

### Tips on Chocolate
*Melting Chocolate*
● Chocolate scorches easily, so melt it over hot, not boiling, water. A double boiler is best, but you can improvise by using a cup or bowl in a small saucepan. Either way, keep the water just below simmering. If steam gets into melting chocolate it will thicken the mixture and make it difficult to mix with the other ingredients. However, if this happens, simply soften the chocolate by adding 1 to 2 tablespoons vegetable shortening (not butter) and stir vigorously.

● If there is liquid in a chocolate recipe such as milk, water or spirits, melt the chocolate in the liquid in a small saucepan over direct heat. There should be at least ¼ cup liquid for every 6 ounces chocolate. Stir constantly while melting to blend with liquid.

You can also melt chocolate with the fat in the recipe directly over very low heat. Use a heavy saucepan and watch mixture carefully.

*Storing Chocolate*
When chocolate is stored in too warm a place, or during hot weather, it often develops a whitish film known as "bloom." This is caused by the cocoa butter rising to the surface. It will not affect the eating quality. Chocolate keeps best stored at a temperature of from 60°F. to 70°F, with a low humidity factor.

*Storing Cocoa*
Store cocoa in a tightly covered container at moderate temperature and humidity to keep it from forming lumps or hardening.

### Decorating with Chocolate
Cakes, pies, cookies, candies, puddings and ice-cream desserts take on a professional look with a garnish of grated chocolate or chocolate curls.

*To grate:* Start with cold chocolate, a dry cold grater and cold hands. Rub the square up and down over the grating surface, working quickly and handling the chocolate as little as possible.

*To make curls:* Warm a square of chocolate slightly at room temperature; then, for little curls, shave thin strips from the narrow side with a vegetable parer; for large ones, from the bottom. Pick up the curls with a wooden pick (otherwise they shatter) and chill until firm before arranging on food.

*For fancy chocolate cut-outs* to use as decorations, follow directions for melting and cooling chocolate given in recipe for Chocolate Meringue Torte, which follows, then cut shapes with cookie cutters.

### CHOCOLATE FONDUE
Makes 2½ cups.
- **2 bars (8 ounces each) milk chocolate candy**
- **¾ to 1 cup heavy cream**
- **3 tablespoons brandy**
  **For dipping: strawberries, pear and apple slices, seedless grapes, banana chunks, tangerine and orange sections, pound cake squares, angel food cake squares**

1. Combine chocolate candy and ¾ cup heavy cream in a heavy saucepan. Cook over low heat, stirring constantly, until chocolate is melted. Add brandy. Remove from heat.
2. Pour into small fondue pot; surround by fruit and cake. Spear pieces of fruit or cake on fondue forks; twirl into sauce; provide small plates to catch drippings. If mixture becomes too thick, stir in additional cream.

### CHOCOLATE MERINGUE TORTE
Bake at 300° for 30 minutes.
Makes 10 servings.
**Meringue Layers:**
- **3 egg whites, at room temperature**
- **⅛ teaspoon cream of tartar**
- **¾ cup superfine sugar**
  **Chocolate Curls**
  **(recipe follows)**

**Chocolate Filling:**
- **1 cup heavy cream**
- **5 squares semisweet chocolate**
- **2 squares unsweetened chocolate**
- **2 tablespoons butter or margarine**
- **¾ cup superfine sugar**
- **3 egg whites**
  **10X (confectioners') sugar**

1. Prepare Layers: Grease 1 large and 1 small cookie sheet; dust with flour, tapping off excess. Using an 8-inch layer-cake pan as a guide, draw two 8-inch circles on large cookie

sheet and one on small one. Preheat oven to 300°.

2. Beat the 3 egg whites with cream of tartar until foamy-white and double in volume in large bowl with electric mixer. Sprinkle in ¾ cup sugar, 1 tablespoon at a time, beating all the time until sugar dissolves completely and meringue stands in firm peaks. (Beating will take about 15 minutes in all with an electric mixer.) Spoon mixture evenly onto the 3 circles; spread out to edge.

3. Bake in a preheated slow oven (300°) for 30 minutes or until layers are firm and lightly golden. Cool 5 minutes on cookie sheets on wire racks, then loosen meringue layers carefully with a wide spatula and slide onto racks; cool.

4. Make Chocolate Curls.

5. Prepare Filling: Heat cream in top of double boiler; add semisweet and unsweetened chocolate. Stir often with a wooden spoon until chocolate is completely melted. Stir in butter and ¼ cup of remaining sugar.

6. Beat remaining 3 egg whites until foamy-white in large bowl with electric mixer; gradually add remaining ½ cup sugar, beating well after each addition; continue beating until meringue is glossy and stands in firm peaks.

7. Partly fill bottom of double boiler with ice and water; set top of boiler with chocolate mixture in ice water. Beat chocolate mixture at high speed with electric mixer or rotary hand beater until light and fluffy and almost double in volume; scrape down sides of double boiler often. Fold chocolate into meringue until no streaks of white or brown remain.

8. Place 1 meringue layer on a serving plate; spread with about 1 cup chocolate filling; repeat with another layer and 1 cup filling. Place third layer on top. Frost sides and top with remaining filling. Arrange prepared Chocolate Curls on top of cake; chill. Thirty minutes before serving, remove cake from refrigerator for ease in serving; sprinkle lightly with 10X sugar. Cut in wedges with sharp serrated knife.

**Chocolate Curls**: Melt 6 squares semisweet chocolate in a small bowl over hot water, stirring often. Turn out onto cold cookie sheet. It will spread naturally to about ¼-inch thick. Cool until set. Pull a long metal spatula at a 45-degree angle across chocolate, letting the chocolate curl up in front of the spatula. Place curls on wax paper. It takes a little practice, so count on a few to be less than perfect; put these on the cake first. Makes enough curls to decorate an 8- or 9-inch cake.

## CHOCOLATE FUDGE CAKE

Bake at 350° for 35 minutes.
Makes one 9-inch cake.

- **3 squares unsweetened chocolate**
- **2¼ cups *sifted* cake flour**
- **2 teaspoons baking soda**
- **½ teaspoon salt**
- **½ cup (1 stick) butter or margarine**
- **2¼ cups firmly packed light brown sugar**
- **3 large eggs**
- **1½ teaspoons vanilla**
- **1 cup dairy sour cream**
- **1 cup boiling water**
  **Chocolate Fudge Frosting (recipe follows)**

1. Melt chocolate in a small bowl over hot, not boiling, water; cool.
2. Grease and flour two 9 × 1½-inch layer-cake pans; tap out excess flour. (Or, use cocoa in place of flour to keep cake dark on outside.)
3. Sift flour, baking soda and salt onto wax paper. Preheat oven to 350°.
4. Beat butter until soft in large bowl. Add brown sugar and eggs; beat with electric mixer at high speed until light and fluffy, 5 minutes. Beat in vanilla and cooled melted chocolate.
5. Stir in dry ingredients alternately with sour cream, beating well with a wooden spoon after each addition until batter is smooth. Stir in boiling water. (Batter will be thin.) Pour at once into prepared pans.
6. Bake in a preheated moderate oven (350°) for 35 minutes or until centers spring back when lightly pressed with fingertip.

7. Cool layers in pans on wire rack, 10 minutes; loosen around edges with a small knife or spatula; turn out onto wire racks; cool completely.

8. Prepare Chocolate Fudge Frosting. Place one cake layer on a serving plate; spread with about one-quarter of frosting; place second layer over. Gently brush off loose crumbs and spread a thin coat of frosting over top and sides; let set. Spread remaining frosting, making swirls with spatula.

## CHOCOLATE FUDGE FROSTING

Makes enough to fill and frost two 9-inch layers.

- **4 squares unsweetened chocolate**
- **½ cup (1 stick) butter or margarine**
- **1 package (1 pound) 10X (confectioners') sugar**
- **½ cup milk**
- **2 teaspoons vanilla**

1. Combine chocolate and butter in small heavy saucepan. Cook over low heat just until melted; remove.
2. Combine 10X sugar, milk and vanilla in medium-size bowl; stir until smooth; add chocolate mixture.
3. Set bowl in pan of ice and water; beat with wooden spoon until frosting is thick enough to spread and hold its shape.

## CHOCOLATE FUDGE SAUCE

*Serve over ice cream or cake.*
Makes 2 cups.

- **1 package (6 ounces) semisweet chocolate pieces**
- **1 can (14 ounces) sweetened condensed milk (not evaporated milk)**
- **1 teaspoon vanilla**
  **Pinch salt**
- **⅓ cup hot water**

1. Melt chocolate pieces in top of double boiler over simmering water. Add condensed milk, vanilla and salt, stirring constantly until mixture is slightly thickened. Stir in water.
2. Let cool; cover and refrigerate. If too thick, stir in hot water, 1 tablespoon at a time.

# Chocolate

## BRAZILIAN CHOCOLATE ROLL

Bake at 375° for 12 minutes.
Makes one 10-inch roll.

- ¾ cup *sifted* cake flour
- ¼ cup unsweetened cocoa powder
- 1 teaspoon baking powder
- ¼ teaspoon salt
- 3 eggs
- 1 cup granulated sugar
- ⅓ cup strong cold coffee
- 1 teaspoon vanilla
  10X (confectioners') sugar
  Coffee Cream Filling *(recipe follows)*
  Chocolate Glaze *(recipe follows)*
  Chopped pistachio nuts

1. Grease a 15½ × 10½ × 1-inch jelly-roll pan; line bottom with wax paper; grease paper. Preheat oven to 375°.
2. Sift flour, cocoa, baking powder and salt onto a piece of wax paper.
3. Beat eggs in a medium-size bowl with an electric mixer until thick and creamy. Gradually add sugar while continuing to beat until mixture is very thick and light. Stir in coffee and vanilla. Fold in flour mixture. Spread batter evenly in prepared pan.
4. Bake in a preheated moderate oven (375°) for 12 minutes or until center springs back when lightly pressed with fingertip.
5. Loosen cake around edges; invert onto clean towel which has been liberally sprinkled with 10X sugar. Peel off wax paper. Trim ¼ inch from all 4 sides for easy rolling. Starting at short end, roll up cake *and* towel together. Place, seam-side down, on wire rack; cool completely.
6. Prepare Coffee Cream Filling.
7. Unroll cake carefully; spread evenly with filling. Reroll cake and filling by lifting towel at short end and tucking under first turn, then letting cake roll over on itself. Place, seam-side down, on serving plate.
8. Prepare Chocolate Glaze: Reserve 1 tablespoon of the glaze for decorating; spread remaining glaze evenly over cake. Drizzle reserved glaze over; sprinkle with pistachio nuts; refrigerate until serving time.

**Coffee Cream Filling**: Combine 1 cup heavy cream, 2 teaspoons instant coffee and ¼ cup 10X sugar in a medium-size bowl. Beat with electric mixer until stiff. Makes 2 cups.

**Chocolate Glaze**: Melt 1 square unsweetened chocolate and 1 tablespoon butter or margarine in a small saucepan over low heat. Remove from heat; stir in ½ cup 10X sugar and 2 tablespoons boiling water until smooth. Spread on cooled cake while still warm. Makes ⅓ cup.

## DEEP DARK DEVIL'S FOOD CAKE

Bake at 350° for 40 minutes.
Makes one 9-inch cake.

- 2 cups *sifted* cake flour
- ⅔ cup unsweetened cocoa powder
- ¾ teaspoon baking powder
- 1¼ teaspoons baking soda
- 1 teaspoon salt
- ⅔ cup vegetable shortening
- 1⅓ cups sugar
- 3 large eggs
- 2 teaspoons vanilla
- 1¼ cups water
  Fluffy 7-Minute Frosting *(recipe follows)*
- 1 square unsweetened chocolate
- 1 tablespoon butter or margarine

1. Sift flour, cocoa, baking powder, baking soda and salt onto wax paper. Preheat oven to 350°.
2. Beat shortening, sugar, eggs and vanilla in a large bowl with electric mixer at high speed until fluffy-light, about 5 minutes. Beat in flour mixture alternately with water on low speed. Do not overbeat. Pour into two greased 9 × 1½-inch layer-cake pans.
3. Bake in a preheated moderate oven (350°) for 40 minutes or until centers spring back when lightly pressed with fingertip. Cool in pans on wire rack for 10 minutes. Remove from pans; cool.
4. Make Fluffy 7-Minute Frosting. Place 1 cake layer on a serving plate; spread with about ¼ of the frosting; place second layer over. Gently brush off loose crumbs and spread a thin coat of frosting over top and sides; let set. Spread remaining frosting, making swirls with spatula.

5. Melt chocolate square with the butter in a cup over hot water; stir until smooth. Drizzle over top of cake, letting mixture drip down side, if you wish.

## FLUFFY 7-MINUTE FROSTING

Makes enough to fill and frost two 8- or 9-inch cake layers.

- 1½ cups sugar
- ¼ cup water
- 2 egg whites
- 2 tablespoons light corn syrup
- ¼ teaspoon salt
- 1 teaspoon vanilla

1. Combine sugar, water, egg whites, corn syrup and salt in top of double boiler; beat mixture until well blended.
2. Place over simmering water; cook, beating constantly at high speed with electric hand mixer or rotary beater, about 7 minutes or until mixture triples in volume and holds firm peaks. Remove from heat; beat in vanilla. Spread on cooled cake while still warm.

——————— ●●● ———————

**CHOWDER** A hearty soup made from a variety of ingredients, although it is most often made from seafood and milk. The word "chowder" is taken from the French word *chaudière,* a large heavy kettle used in making soups and stews.

## FISH AND POTATO CHOWDER

Makes 4 servings.

- ½ cup diced salt pork
- 1½ cups frozen chopped onions
- 2 cans (16 ounces each) diced or sliced potatoes
- 1 bay leaf
- ½ teaspoon salt
- ½ teaspoon leaf savory, crumbled
- ¼ teaspoon white pepper
- ⅛ teaspoon leaf thyme, crumbled
- 1 package (1 pound) frozen cod fillets, thawed
- 1½ cups milk

1. Place salt pork and onions in Dutch oven or large kettle. Cook over high heat until pork has begun to brown and liquid has evaporated from onions.

2. Add potatoes with can liquid, bay leaf, salt, savory, pepper and thyme. Cover; cook over high heat 5 minutes.

3. Meanwhile, pat fish between paper toweling to remove excess liquid. Cut into 1-inch cubes. Add to Dutch oven; cover; cook gently 3 minutes. Add milk and heat to simmer.

## SAVORY CLAM CHOWDER

*Thyme adds its pungent good taste to this hearty chowder that is a variation of the popular Manhattan.*

Makes 6 servings.

- 1 **can (28 ounces) tomatoes**
- 4 **large carrots, pared and sliced**
- 2 **cups chopped celery**
- 2 **large onions, chopped (2 cups)**
- 1 **teaspoon salt**
- ¼ **teaspoon pepper**
- 4 **cups water**
- 24 **fresh clams (with juice), chopped**
  OR: 2 **cans (8½ ounces each) minced clams and 1 bottle (8 ounces) clam broth**
- 1 **package (10 ounces) frozen lima beans**
- ¼ **cup bacon drippings**
- ¼ **cup all-purpose flour**
- 1 **tablespoon chopped fresh thyme**

1. Combine tomatoes, carrots, celery, onions, salt, pepper and water in a large kettle; bring to boiling. Lower heat and cover kettle; simmer 40 minutes.

2. Stir in clams, broth and lima beans; simmer 10 minutes.

3. Blend bacon drippings and flour in a cup to make a roux. Drop by spoonfuls into hot liquid; add thyme. Cook, stirring constantly, until mixture thickens slightly and bubbles, 3 minutes. Serve with chowder crackers, if you wish.

*Note:* When substituting dried leaf thyme for fresh: Measure ¼ cup of the tomato liquid into a cup. Crumble 1 teaspoon thyme into liquid; let stand 15 minutes. Add thyme and tomato liquid to chowder when adding roux.

— ●●● —

**CHRISTMAS FOOD GIFTS** Your own, homemade food can make a very special gift. Edible gifts can be sweet or savory. They include candies, cookies, fabulous cheese spreads, steamed pudding, flavored mustards, fruitcakes, even your special sauce or spice blends. Pack them into pretty containers or jars for gift-giving. For more recipes, see **BREAD, CANDY, COOKIE, FRUITCAKE.**

## CARROT-PINEAPPLE MARMALADE

Makes 4 half pints.

- 2 **lemons**
- ½ **pound carrots, shredded (2 cups)**
- 2 **cups water**
- 1¾ **cups sugar**
- 1 **can (15¼ ounces) crushed pineapple in pineapple juice**
- ½ **6-ounce package liquid pectin**

1. Shred rind from lemons, about ¼ cup, and combine with carrots in large saucepan.

2. Squeeze juice from lemons, about ⅓ cup; add to saucepan with water. Simmer 20 minutes until tender.

3. Stir in sugar and pineapple; bring to a full boil; boil 1 minute, stirring constantly. Remove from heat; stir in liquid pectin (1 pouch).

4. Skim off foam and stir about 8 minutes to cool. Ladle into 4 hot 8-ounce jars; seal. Process 10 minutes in *simmering* water bath (185°). Cool; label and store in cool, dry place.

## BASIC FRENCH MUSTARD

Makes 1 cup.

- ¼ **cup dry mustard**
- 1 **tablespoon sugar**
- ½ **teaspoon salt**
- ⅓ **cup dry white wine**
- ¼ **cup white wine vinegar**
- 3 **egg yolks**

1. Combine mustard, sugar and salt in a small saucepan. Stir in wine and wine vinegar until smooth. Let stand, uncovered, for 2 hours.

2. Beat egg yolks in a small bowl until light. Stir into mustard mixture. Cook over low heat, stirring constantly, until slightly thickened, about 5 minutes. Do not allow to boil. Cool; pour into small jars; cover. May be stored in refrigerator for up to 1 month. Use as is or as a base for Tomato Mustard.

**Tomato Mustard:** Add 1 teaspoon paprika and 4 tablespoons tomato paste with the egg yolks. Nice with shrimp, hamburgers, frankfurters, and baked ham.

## SWEET 'N' HOT MUSTARD

Makes 1 cup.

- 1 **medium-size onion, finely chopped (½ cup)**
- 1 **clove garlic, minced**
- 1 **cup dry white wine**
- ⅔ **cup dry mustard**
- 1½ **teaspoons vegetable oil**
- 1 **tablespoon honey**
- 1 **teaspoon salt**
- 2 **to 3 drops liquid hot pepper seasoning**

1. Combine onion, garlic and wine in a small saucepan. Bring to boiling; lower heat; simmer 5 minutes.

2. Pour mixture into a small bowl; cool. Strain wine mixture into dry mustard in a small saucepan, beating constantly until smooth. Beat in oil, honey, salt and pepper seasoning.

3. Cook over low heat, stirring constantly, until mixture thickens. Cool; pour into small jars; cover.

4. May be stored in refrigerator for up to 1 month.

## LEMON CURD

Makes about 4½ cups.

- 2 **whole eggs**
- 2 **egg yolks**
- 1½ **cups sugar**
- 2 **tablespoons grated lemon rind**
- ⅔ **cup lemon juice**
- 1 **cup (2 sticks) butter or margarine, melted**

Beat eggs, yolks and sugar in the top of a double boiler with electric mixer until light and fluffy, 3 to 5 minutes. Beat in rind, juice and butter. Cook, stirring constantly, over hot, not boiling, water until mixture thickens, about 15 minutes. Remove from heat; cool. Spoon into jars; seal; refrigerate for up to 2 weeks.

Overleaf: (Counterclockwise from top center) Deep Dark Devil's Food Cake, page 186; Chocolate Meringue Torte, page 184; Chocolate Fudge Cake, page 185; Brazilian Chocolate Roll, page 186.

# Christmas Food Gifts

## CRANBERRY-APPLE GLAZE

Makes 2 cups.

- **2 cups cranberry-apple drink**
- **2 tablespoons cornstarch**
- **1 teaspoon Worcestershire sauce**
- **8 whole cloves**

1. Blend ¼ cup of the cranberry drink into cornstarch in small cup. Stir into remaining cranberry drink in small saucepan. Add Worcestershire sauce and cloves.
2. Bring to boiling, stirring constantly, 1 minute until thickened. Remove from heat. Cool and pour into containers. Refrigerate, covered, up to a week.
3. To use: Stir gently. Brush over ham or spareribs for last 40 minutes of baking.

## APRICOT-ORANGE WINTER BARBECUE SAUCE

Makes 1½ cups.

- **1 medium-size onion, chopped (½ cup)**
- **1 clove garlic, minced**
- **2 tablespoons vegetable oil**
- **1 can (17 ounces) apricot halves**
- **¼ cup cider vinegar**
- **3 tablespoons undiluted frozen orange juice concentrate**
- **3 tablespoons light brown sugar**
- **1 teaspoon dry mustard**
- **½ teaspoon ground ginger**
- **½ teaspoon salt**
- **3 to 4 drops liquid hot pepper seasoning**

1. Sauté onion and garlic in oil in a medium-size saucepan until tender, about 5 minutes.
2. Drain apricot halves (reserve syrup for gelatin dessert). Place in container of electric blender; cover. Whirl just until smooth. Add cider vinegar, orange juice concentrate, brown sugar, mustard, ginger, salt and hot pepper seasoning. Cover; whirl just until blended.
3. Stir mixture into onion; bring to boiling, stirring constantly. Lower heat; simmer, uncovered, until mix-

ture thickens, about 15 minutes. Cool before storing in containers. Refrigerate for up to 2 weeks.

4. To use: Serve with broiled or roasted meats or brush over chicken pieces before baking, or brush over ham or spareribs for last 30 minutes of baking.

## LEMON-LIME MARMALADE

Makes 5 half pints.

- **3 large lemons**
- **6 limes**
- **6 cups water**
- **5 cups sugar**
- **¼ cup shredded preserved ginger**

1. Wash, seed and slice thinly 2 of the lemons and 3 of the limes. Pack tightly to make 1½ cups.
2. Use vegetable parer to remove rind (colored part only, no white) from remaining lemon and 3 limes. Cut into thin strips 1/16-inch wide and 2-inches long to make ½ cup.
3. Place slices and rind in large kettle with water. Bring to boiling; boil 20 minutes. Stir in sugar and ginger. Boil 20 more minutes until jelly sheets from cold metal spoon.
4. Skim off foam; ladle into 5 hot 8-ounce jars. Seal.
5. Process 10 minutes in *simmering* water bath (185°). Cool; label and store in a cool, dry place.

## STRAWBERRY-ORANGE MARMALADE

Makes 5 half pints.

- **3 oranges**
- **2 lemons**
- **6 cups water**
- **4 cups sugar**
- **1 bag (1 pound) frozen whole unsweetened strawberries, partially thawed**

1. Cut 2 oranges into quarters; remove seeds. Slice thinly (about 2 cups).
2. Cut 1 lemon in half lengthwise; slice thinly, removing seeds.
3. Remove rind from remaining orange and lemon with vegetable parer. Cut into thin strips 1/16-inch wide and 2-inches long.
4. Combine slices and rind in large

kettle with water. Bring to boiling; boil 30 minutes until soft.

5. Combine sugar and strawberries in large bowl; mash slightly; stir into kettle. Boil 30 more minutes until liquid sheets from spoon.
6. Skim off foam; ladle into 5 hot 8-ounce jars. Seal. Process 10 minutes in *simmering* water bath (185°). Cool; label and store in cool, dry place.

## PAPAYA CHUTNEY

Makes 9 half pints.

- **2 large papayas (3 pounds total), pared, seeded and chopped (about 5 cups)**
- **2 large onions, chopped (2 cups)**
- **3 apples, pared and chopped (3 cups)**
- **1 cup golden raisins**
- **1 sweet red pepper, chopped (1 cup)**
- **1½ teaspoons mustard seeds**
- **1 cup cider vinegar**
- **2 cups sugar**
- **2 teaspoons salt**
- **¼ cup shredded preserved ginger**

1. Combine all ingredients in kettle or Dutch oven. Bring to boiling, stirring often; lower heat and simmer 30 minutes until mixture is thickened. Stir often to prevent scorching.
2. Ladle into 9 hot 8-ounce jars leaving ¼-inch head space. Seal jars. Process for 10 minutes in boiling water bath (212°). Cool; check seals; label and store in cool, dry place.

———————— •••  ————————

**CHUTNEY** This accompaniment to curry dishes is made from a mixture of fresh fruit (usually mango), dried fruit (such as raisins) and spices. Chutney, which is of Indian origin, can also be served as a relish with poultry, pork or ham. For a recipe, see **CHRISTMAS FOOD GIFTS**.

**CINNAMON** Cinnamon is the bark of several varieties of an evergreen tree native to Southeast Asia. True cinnamon is the Ceylon variety; others are from cassia trees.

Ceylon cinnamon is native to Ceylon and India. It has the mildest

Pictured opposite: Christmas Food Gifts, pages 187 and 190

# Citron

tasting bark and for that reason is not popular in this country. It is used extensively in Mexico. Americans prefer the stronger taste of the bark from the cassia trees. One variety, the Saigon cassia, originated in China but is now grown extensively in Indo-China. This variety is ground. Another variety, the Batavia cassia, is rolled into sticks.

Cinnamon or cassia bark is harvested by cutting the young shoots of the tree. The bark is stripped and scraped. The inner bark, which is the fragrant layer, folds into itself when it starts to dry out and looks like a roll of paper. It is rolled until about ½ inch in diameter and can be up to 3 feet long. Cinnamon sticks and ground cinnamon are widely used. Oil of cinnamon is extracted from the berries of the tree and also the residue of the bark. The oil is used for flavoring candies and desserts.

**CITRON** The citron is a thick-skinned citrus fruit; it resembles a lemon but is about 6 inches long. It was originally found growing in the Himalayas, but the natives there could not find a use for it. When it was then taken to Italy, the peel was candied. Candied citron peel is used in fruitcakes and cookies and is available diced or in halved pieces.

**CITRUS** The juicy fruits of citrus trees are familiar to everyone. These fruits, rich in vitamin C, grow in warm climates around the world. Most of them originated in Southeast Asia and China in particular. When selecting citrus fruits, look for firm, unblemished skins.

### Citrus Tips
● To get the most juice from the fruit, store at room temperature. Roll the fruit firmly between your hand and the counter before squeezing.
● Extra grated citrus rind can be frozen in sealed plastic bags. Use as you would fresh grated rind.
● Save citrus shells after juicing; freeze and use later as serving containers for relishes, dips, sauces, salads or desserts.

For more information, see **CITRON, GRAPEFRUIT, KUMQUAT, LEMON, LIME, ORANGE, TANGELO, TANGERINE** and **UGLI FRUIT**.

**CLAMS** Clams are bivalved mollusks. Many varieties are found along the Atlantic, Pacific and Gulf coasts. Clams were abundant and cheap in colonial America and widely used in many dishes. They may be fried, served raw on the half-shell, steamed or used to make chowders or fritters.

**Buying**: *Softshell clams* are found from the Arctic Ocean to Cape Hatteras. These small clams have a black-skinned neck or siphon and are a favorite when steamed.

*Hardshell clams* are known by their Indian name "quahaug" or "quahog." Small quahogs are called *Little Necks*, named after Long Island's Little Neck Bay. A larger size quahog is known as *Cherrystones* for Cherrystone Creek in Virginia. Little Neck and Cherrystone clams are served raw on the half-shell or cooked. Larger quahogs are marketed for chowder or fritters.

*Razor clams* are very large clams that look like an old-fashioned razor. Different species are found along each coast. Razor clams are usually cut up and cooked.

Clams are available in the shell or shucked and canned, either whole or minced. When fresh, they are sold by the dozen; buy only clams with tightly closed shells. Refrigerate and use within 2 days. Bottled clam juice is available to use in making soups and chowders.

**To Prepare**: Fresh clams should be placed in a container of salted water (⅓ cup salt to 1 gallon water) mixed with ¼ cup cornmeal for several hours so that they will cleanse themselves of sand. Scrub clams well with a stiff brush. Use a clam knife to open them.

## RHODE ISLAND CLAM CHOWDER
Makes 6 servings.
- ¼ **pound salt pork, diced**
- 1 **medium-size onion, sliced**
- 4 **cups diced potatoes**

- 1 **quart clams, drained, picked over and chopped (reserve juice)**
- 2 **teaspoons salt**
- ¼ **teaspoon white pepper**
  **Reserved clam juice, plus boiling water to make**
- 2½ **cups**
  **Oyster crackers**

Fry the salt pork in a skillet until brown. Remove bits to a side dish and reserve. Fry the onion in the salt pork fat, drain onion and add to reserved pork bits. Place diced potatoes in a large pot, add chopped clams, sprinkle with salt and pepper. Add the boiling water and reserved clam juice and cook, covered, 10 to 15 minutes or until potatoes are tender. Add salt pork bits and onion and simmer 10 minutes or so. Serve with oyster crackers.

———— ●●● ————

**CLAY COOKERY** Clay and earthenware have been used as cooking vessels for thousands of years. Cooking in clay has several advantages. Foods may be cooked without added fat. They cook in their own juices, retaining nutrients and staying moist and juicy.

Unglazed clay pots are available from several manufacturers in different shapes and sizes. The usual procedure for cooking in a clay pot is to submerge the top and bottom in water for a few minutes. Then the pot is filled with the food and placed in a cold oven, which is then turned on to a very high temperature.

**CLOVES** Both whole and ground cloves are used extensively in a variety of foods.

Cloves are the dried flower buds of an evergreen tree, which grows to a height of 40 feet and blooms year-round. The flower buds are first white, then turn green and finally a bright red, ready for picking. They are picked and then dried, which turns them a dark brown color. The bulbous end of a clove is the unopened flower. Since a clove looks like a nail, it received its name from the French word *clou*, meaning "nail."